PERSIANS: MASTERS OF EMPIRE

Time-Life Books is a division of Time Life Inc.

PRESIDENT and CEO: John M. Fahey Jr.

EDITOR-IN-CHIEF: John L. Papanek

TIME-LIFE BOOKS

MANAGING EDITOR: Roberta Conlan

Director of Design: Michael Hentges
Director of Editorial Operations: Ellen Robling
Director of Photography and Research: John Conrad Weiser
Senior Editors: Russell B. Adams Jr., Dale M. Brown, Janet Cave, Lee Hassig, Robert Somerville, Henry Woodhead
Special Projects Editor: Rita Thievon Mullin
Director of Technology: Eileen Bradley
Library: Louise D. Forstall

PRESIDENT: John D. Hall

Vice President, Director of Marketing: Nancy K. Jones
Vice President, Director of New Product Development: Neil Kagan
Vice President, Book Production: Marjann Caldwell
Production Manager: Marlene Zack
Quality Assurance Manager: James King

**Library of Congress
Cataloging in Publication Data**
Persians: masters of empire / by the editors of Time-Life Books.

p. cm. —(Lost civilizations)
Includes bibliographical references and index.
ISBN 0-8094-9104-4
1. Iran—Antiquities.
2. Iran—History—To 640.
I. Time-Life Books. II. Series.
DS261.P47 1995
935—dc20 95-13943
CIP

LOST CIVILIZATIONS

SERIES EDITOR: Dale M. Brown

Administrative Editor: Philip Brandt George

Editorial staff for *Persians: Masters of Empire*

Art Director: Bill McKenney

Picture Editor: Marion Ferguson Briggs

Text Editors: Charlotte Anker (principal), Russell B. Adams Jr., Charles J. Hagner

Associate Editors/Research-Writing: Katherine L. Griffin, Mary Grace Mayberry, Jarelle S. Stein

Senior Copyeditor: Barbara Fairchild Quarmby

Picture Coordinator: Catherine Parrott

Editorial Assistant: Patricia D. Whiteford

Special Contributors: Anthony Allan, Ellen Galford, Jimmy L. Hicks, Ellen Phillips (text); Rita T. Mullin, Eugenia S. Scharf, Ylann Schemm (research); Roy Nanovic (index)

Correspondents: Christine Hinze (London), Christina Lieberman (New York), Maria Vincenza Aloisi (Paris). Valuable assistance was also provided by: Mehmet Ali Kislali (Ankara); John Dunn (Australia); Angelica Lemmer (Bonn); Gay Kavanagh (Brussels); Judy Aspinall (London); Constance Richards (Moscow); Meenakshi Ganguly (New Delhi); Elizabeth Brown (New York); Ann Natanson and Ann Wise (Rome); Robert Kroon (Switzerland); Traudl Lessing (Vienna).

The Consultants:

Carol Bier, curator of the Eastern Hemisphere Collections at the Textile Museum in Washington, D.C., has served as a consultant to the Brooklyn Museum, Dumbarton Oaks, the Royal Ontario Museum, and the Smithsonian Institution, among others. Author of numerous articles on Middle Eastern textiles, Bier has done extensive fieldwork in Syria, Jordan, Lebanon, Egypt, Iran, and Turkey.

Robert Carl Henrickson is a research collaborator in the Conservations Analytical Laboratory of the Smithsonian Institution, concentrating in Near Eastern Archaeology. An expert in the production and distribution of pottery, intrasettlement residential patterns, and the evolution and dynamics of complex societies, he aided with the early development and planning for this volume.

Holly Pittman, curator of Ancient Near Eastern Art at the Metropolitan Museum of Art for 14 years, is associate professor of Art History at the University of Pennsylvania, where she specializes in the ancient Near East. She has done extensive fieldwork in Cyprus, Iran, Iraq, and Syria, and most recently at a late-fourth-century-BC site in eastern Turkey.

Michael Roaf, former director of the British School of Archaeology in Iraq and an associate professor at the University of California, Berkeley, is professor of Near Eastern Archaeology at the University of Munich, Germany. He has excavated exhaustively in Iran, including five seasons at the Median site of Tepe Nush-i Jan, as well as in Iraq, Bahrain, Egypt, and Greece. In addition to writing numerous articles, he is the author of the *Cultural Atlas of Mesopotamia and the Ancient Near East*.

This volume is one in a series that explores the worlds of the past, using the finds of archaeologists and other scientists to bring ancient peoples and their cultures vividly to life.

PERSIANS: MASTERS OF EMPIRE

By the Editors of Time-Life Books

TIME-LIFE BOOKS, ALEXANDRIA, VIRGINIA

CONTENTS

CASPIAN SEA

Oxus River

Nysa •

GOLD CHARIOT

UNTAINS

ran

DESERT

e Sialk

TOMB OF CYRUS

DESERT

• Shahr-i Sokhte

N

•Pasargadae
•Persepolis

• Anshan

Bishapur

•Taoke
Gur•

• Shahdad

•Tepe Yahya

PRINCE'S HEAD

GULF

GULF OF OMAN

TIME ®
LIFE
BOOKS

Cover: The serene visage of a young Persian prince is bracketed by royal guards on one of the stairways at Persepolis, the royal city built by Darius I. Persepolis stands as an enduring monument to the kings who ruled the Persian empire from the mid-sixth century BC to 330 BC, when Alexander the Great defeated Darius III.

End paper: Painted by artist Paul Breeden, the map highlights sites and cities important in the development of ancient Persia. The icons represent influential cultures and empires between 4000 BC and the seventh century AD. The shaded area of the inset shows the geographical extent of the Persian empire under Darius I (522-486 BC), with the red line tracing the 1,600-mile route of the Persian-built Royal Road, a wonder of its time. Breeden also provided the vignettes for the timeline on pages 158-159.

HOW THE LAND OF THE GODS BECAME THE LAND OF THE PERSIANS

Sometime around 647 BC, Elam, a mighty kingdom in what is today western Iran, fell to its enemy, the Assyrians. When its vanquisher, Ashurbanipal, returned in triumph to Nineveh in present-day Iraq, he summoned a scribe to record his victory. His gloating words might have disappeared into the void had he not had them inscribed in cuneiform on a 13-inch-long, six-sided cylinder of baked clay that was placed ceremoniously in a wall of the palace. There, some 2,400 years later in 1854, Iraqi Hormuzd Rassam, chief assistant to Nineveh's British excavator, Henry Austen Layard, freed the prism from its ancient hiding place. The discovery so excited Rassam that he proceeded to rip down every wall he could find in the palace that might conceal other writings.

The text that provoked such zeal reveals Ashurbanipal as an avenger seeking retribution for the humiliations the Elamites had inflicted on the Mesopotamians over the centuries: "Susa, the great holy city, abode of their gods, seat of their mysteries, I conquered. I entered its palaces, I dwelt there rejoicing; I opened the treasuries where silver and gold, goods and wealth were amassed . . . the treasures of Sumer, Akkad and Babylon that the ancient kings of Elam had looted and carried away. I destroyed the ziggurat of Susa. I smashed its shining copper horns. I reduced the temples of Elam to naught; their gods and goddesses I scattered to the winds. The tombs of their

From a second-millennium-BC tomb at the Elamite city of Susa, this life-size clay head lay next to a skull and may have been a portrait of the dead man. The Elamites, fierce rivals of the Babylonians, were precursors of the royal Persians.

7

ancient and recent kings I devastated, I exposed to the sun, and I carried away their bones toward the land of Ashur. I devastated the provinces of Elam and on their lands I sowed salt."

A man known for his cruelty, Ashurbanipal used such ruthlessness not just against his enemies but as a psychological threat to the vassal states he held in his thrall. Head of a great empire, he was among the last rulers of a long succession of ancient city-states—Sumer, Akkad, Babylon, Assur—that had dominated the rich alluvial plains between the Tigris and Euphrates Rivers known as Mesopotamia. Yet even as he recounted his victory over the Elamites, the era of Mesopotamian dynasties was waning. Eventually the center of power would shift to the southeast, a terrain of plain and mountains in today's Iran whose peoples were now lamenting the devastation of Susa, their wondrous city.

Susa had long enjoyed an enviable position, straddling as it did the most direct route from the lowland kingdoms to the mountains. It lay about 130 miles north of the Persian Gulf, where the Mesopotamian plain spreads eastward toward a land of extraordinary geographical diversity. Although this land contained two uninhabitable salt deserts, it was rimmed by fertile plateaus. In the north, high mountain passes led into Central Asia. Lesser ranges farther east bordered today's Afghanistan and Pakistan. Midwest reared the Zagros Mountains, looming over a western plain.

The mountain rivers and streams were the source of the water that nourished the high valleys and the oases of the arid interior and, when spread over the fields by irrigation, made it possible for farmers to till the soil. From the soaring peaks also came the raw materials that made Elam wealthy: marble, alabaster, carnelian, lapis

Ashurbanipal's brutal campaign against Elam is triumphantly recorded in this relief from his Nineveh palace showing the sack of an Elamite city in 647 BC. Here flames rise from buildings as Assyrian soldiers topple the city walls with pickaxes and crowbars and carry off the spoils. Their skill in close-quarter fighting enabled the Assyrians to easily overwhelm the Elamites, who were too dependent on bows and arrows for defense.

French archaeologist Jacques de Morgan's excavations of the Susa acropolis were in full swing when Jules-Georges Bondoux, a French artist traveling through Persia in 1905, made his sketches for this painting of the mound that held the remains of the city. The 15-foot-high work—showing some 20th-century wear and tear—captures the pastoral timelessness of wading herons but reveals little of the archaeological drama unfolding in Susa's shadowed mound. The ancient and illustrious city lasted some 5,000 years under a succession of peoples—Elamites, Achaemenids, Seleucids, Parthians, and Muslims—before it was finally destroyed by the Mongols in the 13th century AD.

lazuli, timber, copper, lead, gold, silver, and iron. In the highland folds nestled isolated, fertile valleys, rich in their diversity. And through the passes came peoples who, bringing goods and ideas from elsewhere, helped shape Elamite culture.

In the 3,500-year history that Susa shared with Mesopotamia, the Elamite capital had fallen and risen more than once. It would rise again, when Ashurbanipal himself was dust and his own royal cities had been sacked by his enemies, among them the powers now developing in the land known today as Iran. The name, Iran, means "land of the Aryan" and refers to the Indo-Europeans, or the Aryans, who began migrating into it around 1000 BC. Almost three millennia later Europeans would still refer to much of this region as Persia, a word derived from the province, east of the Persian Gulf, where a group of Indo-Europeans had settled—called Persis by the Greeks. From here this relatively unknown people would launch a series of brilliant campaigns that would make Iran the center of an empire bigger and more powerful than any the world had yet seen.

Within little more than a century after Ashurbanipal's assault, Susa became the glowing city described in the Bible, whose monumental buildings were furnished with "marble pillars and also couches of gold and silver on a mosaic pavement of porphyry, marble, mother of pearl, and precious stones." Indeed the Persian king Darius I, who rebuilt Susa around 518 BC, took care to record that he had adorned Susa with gold from Sardis and Bactria, ivory from Egypt and Ethiopia, and wood from Lebanon—the booty and tribute that came to him as the omnipotent ruler of the Persian empire.

At their height, the Persians controlled nearly two million square miles of territory spreading from Egypt and the Aegean well into India, and from the Persian Gulf to beyond the Black and Caspian Seas. Among their subjects—as evidenced by carved processions seen on its palace facades—were Elamites, Assyrians from Mesopotamia, Ionians and Lydians from Asia Minor, Egyptians and Kushites from Africa, Scythians from the windy Russian Steppe beyond the Black Sea, Armenians from the north, and Bactrians and Indians from the east. The subject peoples' annual payments of gems, metals, spices, fabrics, foodstuffs, animals, and slaves brought in revenues estimated by Herodotus to be worth, at the market value of those times, almost one million pounds of silver.

Rich, ably administered, and highly cultivated, this remarkable empire was governed by a line of kings named after a presumed ancestor, Achaemenes, who may have ruled the Persians in the early seventh century BC. These Achaemenid monarchs, Cyrus and his successors, were men of legendary prowess who issued their decrees from splendid capitals: Susa and Babylon in the lowlands, seven-walled Ecbatana in the mountains, and on the high plains, Pasargadae and Persepolis. But after more than 200 years, in the fourth century BC, the Achaemenids fell to a conqueror whose stature equaled their own, Alexander the Great, the young warrior-king of Macedonia. Their lands then formed the main part of his even larger empire.

Although Alexander's immense domain broke up swiftly after his early death, the core of the territory once under Persian sway survived under one dynasty or another, its lands now growing, now shrinking, for almost 1,000 years. The empire's Persian foundation became overlaid with Greek ideals and Greek culture: first under the rule of Alexander's immediate successors, the Seleucids, from 311 to 141 BC; then under the Parthians, a nomadic people originally from Central Asia, who around 275 BC had migrated into Parthia, the province that lay southeast of the Caspian Sea, and who eventually seized control of the empire. The Parthian dynasty would be followed in AD 224 by a line of monarchs descended from an Iranian ancestor named Sasan. The power of the Sassanians was matched only by that of Rome, of Constantinople, Rome's successor in the East, and of faraway China. The Sassanians fell at last to the Arab armies of Islam, in AD 637, and disappeared from history's stage.

M emories of Persia did not vanish, however, from the realms of the imagination. The Arab conquerors of the region absorbed their Sassanian predecessors' arts and institutions, and even in Europe the books of the Hebrew Bible (Old Testament) and of classical historians, such as Herodotus and Xenophon, preserved the image of the lost world. It was an exotic picture of strange gods and cults, of terrifying excesses and vanished grandeurs, and it had enormous appeal. As early as the 12th century AD, a brave traveler from the West roved as far as Susa; by the 14th century, other Europeans had seen the gaunt columns of ruined Persepolis, the capital of the Achaemenid empire, towering on the Persian plain. This view seemed to represent a bygone barbaric glory. Tales taken back to Europe by visitors caught the public imagination and inspired works as different as English poet Christopher Marlowe's tragedy of 1587, *Tamburlaine the Great,* and composer George Frideric Handel's farcical opera *Xerxes,* first performed in 1738. By the 18th century, more and more Europeans were venturing to Iran, returning with glowing accounts of the ruins, and with copies of mystifying inscriptions at Persepolis and elsewhere, for generations of scholars to pore over.

It was a new imperial age, however, that provided the opportunity for the most significant discoveries in Iran. By the beginning of the 19th century, Western powers had enough commercial interests in the Middle and Far East to send representatives to Iraq, then controlled by the moribund Ottoman Empire. These diplomats, a remarkable breed of scholars, began the archaeological and linguistic work that led to the uncovering of the ancient city-states of Mesopotamia, and to the translation of their long-forgotten languages.

The rich Mesopotamian records enticed scholars eastward into Iran, not only to Persepolis but also to the thousands of tepes, mounds concealing ancient ruins, that lay scattered throughout the vast landscape. There they found the precious remains of former splendors: cities crowded with palaces, temples, and monumental sculpture; writings that revealed the existence of kingdoms reaching far back in time; ornaments, armor, jewelry, and regalia that had been wrought in gold and silver.

The early explorer-archaeologists were also participants in international intrigue, caught up in an unseemly race among European nations for the artifacts of antiquity. They were intrepid, and they had to be. Iran was rugged, daunting terrain. Much of it is high country, at least 1,500 feet above sea level, stretching from the Caspian Sea in the north to the Persian Gulf and the Gulf of Oman in the south. The archaeologists going there tended to work in places inaccessible except by the most perilous of tracks. Some areas were rife with disease, such as malaria. The countryside harbored bandits and murderous, nomadic tribes. Even ordinary Iranians, shepherds or farmers as in ancient times, often harassed the Westerners, whom they saw as unclean infidels. One British report complained that "they refused to sell corn [grain] or sheep to our party; they abused our servants whenever they met; and they kept themselves as far as possible from the contaminating and dreaded influence of the hateful foreigners."

Susa became one of the archaeologists' first targets for investigation in Iran. It was already thousands of years old when the Persians came to power in the sixth century BC. Their leader, the first Persian king, Cyrus, had acknowledged its long, proud Elamite heritage by assuming an Elamite royal title, thus conferring upon himself a noble connection to the past.

While the explorers knew that Elam was an important province of the Persian empire, they had yet to uncover evidence proving just how old Elam—and Susa—actually were. The first to probe the city's ruins was an Englishman named William Kennett Loftus, who arrived in Baghdad in 1849 to serve on the Turco-Persian Boundary Commission, set up by England and Russia to resolve territorial disputes between Iran and the Ottoman Empire, lands that these empire-building nations considered to lie within their

THE ORPHANED STRAYS OF LURISTAN

In the late 1920s, bronze horse trappings, weapons, votive objects, and ornaments began appearing on the international art market in growing numbers. They were being looted from the cemeteries of an apparently seminomadic horse-breeding people who flourished during the first millennium BC in the upland valleys of the Zagros Mountains, a region known as Luristan.

By the mid-1930s, archaeologists such as Erich Schmidt were flying reconnaissance flights over the isolated, rugged heart of Luristan in search of ruins and unopened graves. In 1938, a ninth-century-BC temple site at Surkh Dum yielded hundreds of objects buried in the walls and floors, including the cache of bronze pins with stamped disks seen at right, above. But since Schmidt's findings would remain unpub-

lished for another 50 years, it would be the digging and studies of Belgian archaeologist Louis vanden Berghe that at last provided a stylistic framework for identifying the thousands of "orphaned strays" lying in museums, private collections, and dealers' shops.

Bronze experts like Oscar White Muscarella, at New York's Metropolitan Museum of Art, have used vanden Berghe's research to help authenticate Luristan pieces. He examined the 5½-inch-long pinhead at left, which bore a strong resemblance to a pin recovered at Surkh Dum. He looked for simulated corrosion and patina and for other telltale signs indicating that it might have been cast from an original. He then subjected it to metallographic analysis to determine if the piece was ancient or modern. The pinhead, happily enough, passed the tests.

spheres of national interest. Loftus was a son of his age, confident in his authority as an English officer, a geologist in an era when that science was beginning to change the picture of the earth's history. He was also an archaeologist, sportsman, and adventurer, and the liveliest of observers of the world around him. He was soon sent by the commission chief, another antiquity enthusiast, to identify, map, and excavate Susa.

Loftus set off, after targeting Susa's location based on the books of Genesis, Ezra, Esther, and Daniel in the Old Testament. He also knew the works of the first-century Jewish historian Josephus and of Benjamin of Tudela, who had traveled to Susa in the 12th century AD and described the tomb alleged to be that of the prophet Daniel, which remained a place of pilgrimage even in Loftus's day. And he was familiar with the recently deciphered cuneiform texts.

As Loftus traveled to Susa, by horse and ferry, he recorded all that he saw. Describing the plain he crossed, he observed the lions, wolves, boars, and jackals that populated it. He noted the groves of dates, oranges, and lemons, forests of tamarisk and poplar trees, and fields of rice, indigo, and barley. Once on site, he endured months of high winds and of temperatures that often rose to 120° F., forcing the inhabitants to shelter by day in rooms cut into the earth beneath their houses until they emerged at dusk to sleep outdoors on their flat roofs. He concurred with the view of the first-century Greek geographer Strabo, who commented that Iran was so hot that lizards and snakes could not cross the road for fear of frying. And he enjoyed the delicious relief of the spring season near Susa, where annually the rain-watered land became covered with flowers so beautiful that some people thought the biblical name for the city, Shushan—meaning lilies in Hebrew—must derive from them.

Loftus approached his destination with mounting excitement. From 30 miles away he could see four major mounds, the largest of which covered 60 acres and towered 70 feet. As he drew close, he saw the ruins, still visible above ground, of the apadana, the great columned hall where Persian kings had received the tribute of em-

pire. It was there he began excavating, once he had mapped the site, and came upon fragments of civilizations older still. These included a section of an obelisk bearing 33 lines of cuneiform script, a wall of inscribed bricks, 200 small terra-cotta statues, mainly nude representations of a goddess, and various clay models of animals. The inscribed bricks and the obelisk, Loftus said, were "undoubted proofs of the remote antiquity ascribable to the great Susian citadel." Although he believed there was more to find, Loftus ran out of funds and had to depart, taking with him the artifacts he had discovered, to be preserved in the British Museum.

The French, eager to exploit sites of their own, kept a watchful eye on British work in the region. In 1884, with the modest backing of their government, a husband-and-wife team came to excavate at Susa, the first in a long line of French scholars who would eventually dig there. They were Marcel-Auguste Dieulafoy, a soldier, engineer, and historian of architecture, and his wife, Jane.

The Dieulafoys lived at Susa for two years. Marcel-Auguste produced an imaginative plan reconstructing Achaemenid forts and palaces; he also shipped numerous artifacts to the Louvre, including an enormous bull's head capital from one of the apadana's fallen columns. Jane took back to France the inspiration for several novels—among them *Parysatis,* based on the life of the mother of Cyrus II—and material for two vivacious journals, *An Amazon in the Ori-*

Rifles at the ready, French writer and photographer Jane Dieulafoy rests in the rough open terrain around Susa in this 1886 photograph. During the two years she and her archaeologist husband, Marcel-Auguste, spent excavating the palace of Darius, they were ever wary of marauding tribes. Many of Jane's photographs were later turned into engravings, such as the one at right in which workers crate the Dieulafoys' Achaemenid finds for transport to Paris. The couple's contributions greatly enriched the Louvre's Middle Eastern antiquities collection, which now numbers about 30,000 pieces.

14

ent and *On an Expedition to the Home of the Immortals.* In these works she expressed the sense of fallen majesty that had overwhelmed her at Susa. The very ground under her feet, she wrote, was composed of the dust of ancient monarchies. She also excoriated the less-than-generous monetary backing provided by the parsimonious French government.

Between them, Marcel-Auguste and Jane Dieulafoy helped inspire support for French archaeological interests in Iran. In 1895 the French ambassador at Tehran persuaded Shah Nasir al-Din to grant France the monopoly for archaeological excavation throughout his country, and by 1897, the French government had created the well-funded Delegation Scientifique Française en Perse. In practice, the French stuck mainly to Susa, and the shah's successor agreed in 1900 that every artifact excavated in the alluvial plains region of western Iran, known as Susiana, would go to France, with a stipulated compensation to be paid for the gold and silver items.

The agreement and the way the first excavations were conducted have been matters of controversy from that day to this. Iranians who lived near the excavations proved hostile, and pillaging tribes were so aggressive that the first teams at Susa used some of the ancient bricks and stones at the site to construct, for defense, a castlelike fortification known as the Château. British archaeologist John Curtis called it "the most sumptuous dig house ever constructed." Many archaeologists later expressed outrage, among them Iranians who were naturally offended at being unable to excavate in their own country. One Iranian archaeologist, Ezat Negahban, has ascribed the agreement to the "political and economic confusion of the country and the naiveté of the Iranian government."

Perhaps because of the monopoly granted France and the careless methods employed by the delegation's first head, Jacques de Morgan, the French excavations have since been savagely attacked.

The director was scorned as a treasure hunter who ravaged sites to acquire artifacts for museums. In this he was hardly alone. It is estimated that Morgan and his successors had provided the Louvre with thousands of Elamite artworks, as British archaeologists had the British Museum.

Morgan, however, had approached the project with impressive credentials. An accomplished mining engineer with a deep love for prehistory, he had worked in the Caucasus, in northern Persia, and with great distinction in Egypt, when, at the age of 40, he was made head of the French Archaeological Delegation. For the dig at Susa, he hired a strong team of archaeologists and engineers and set out to uncover the origins of a civilization.

Morgan was handicapped by having little understanding of the architecture of the ancient Middle East and scant knowledge of modern archaeological principles. The houses, palaces, and temples of this ancient world were built from bricks that were mixtures of clay, water, and straw, molded in wooden forms, and dried in the hot sun. Such buildings could easily be demolished in the course of a war, flood, or earthquake; but their impermanency also meant that people had only to flatten out the old structures to provide a platform on which to construct new edifices or even a city. Thus each town rested on its predecessor, and over the years the many layers came to form the high tepes of Iran.

Today the various occupation levels of the tepes are a major source of archaeological knowledge about the life of the people who once inhabited the sites. The aim of modern archaeology, of course, is not simply to recover artifacts but to understand them in their context. This requires careful planning and slow, painstaking work to distinguish the different strata from one another. After his initial

Ensconced in his tapestried study at Susa, Jacques de Morgan looks every bit the proper scholar. The photograph was taken inside the French Archaeological Delegation's headquarters, whose construction he oversaw in the 1890s. Assembled from recycled Elamite and Achaemenid remains, the fortresslike building, dubbed the Château, saved the archaeologists from the physical discomfort and anxiety experienced by the Dieulafoys 15 years earlier. In the foreground of the picture at right runs a portion of Morgan's 300-foot-long "grand trench," which cut a wide swath into Susa's acropolis; in the background is the medieval-looking Château.

explorations at Susa, Morgan decided, much too quickly, that such analysis was impossible. He had anticipated finding at least one large building that would be in good enough shape for the ground plan to be studied. Instead, as he observed in his writings, "I soon realized that everything was in the greatest disorder and that the significant objects, however large, were sparsely distributed among a great deal of rubble."

The Frenchman therefore formed what one commentator calls a "frightening" plan for the fastest, cheapest way to remove the most amount of earth from the main, 115-foot-high mound at Susa. Because he was unable to differentiate the various strata, he divided the mound horizontally into seven 16-foot-deep levels. He said he selected that depth because experience had shown him that when earth was thrown into wagons from a height of 16 feet, the objects hidden in it "would not suffer," a remark that makes contemporary archaeologists shudder. To dig through these layers quickly, he hired 1,200

Almost a foot tall and capable of holding a gallon of liquid, this 6,000-year-old painted vase is considered a masterpiece of prehistoric Iranian pottery, renowned for being decorated with beautifully stylized animals. Thousands of pieces like this one were found by Morgan in the burials of the acropolis cemetery at Susa. Rendered at the site, his sketch (at right, below) illustrates how such bowls and beakers were placed beside the dead.

workmen, far too many for him to supervise effectively or to be able to record the positions of the artifacts uncovered. Irretrievably lost were many of the details that would have provided a chronology of the city's ancient history. Only later, after World War II, when Susa was reexcavated, could a stab be made at assembling such a chronology, with results that were incomplete because of the earlier damage done to the site by Morgan.

What Morgan's haste gave him was a glimpse beneath the Achaemenid city into an older world. He found the elaborate temples of the Elamite kings; tablets covered with the writing known as Proto-Elamite, which was used in the period from 3300 to 2600 BC; and a massive prehistoric cemetery filled with beautifully crafted ceramics. When he left Susa in 1908, exhausted and dispirited by attacks on his work, his assistant, another mining engineer

named Roland de Mecquenem, took over the excavation's direction.

In 1927, Iran terminated the monopoly agreement with France. The French continued their digging but were now joined by archaeological teams from many nations. This intensification of effort led to discoveries at Elamite sites and at the fringes of Elam, revealing a society that, by the time of the Achaemenids, had already been in existence for thousands of years.

Elam's geography gave rise to a culture shaped by two forces. The lowland settlements, such as Susa, were heavily influenced by the urban lifestyle of the bordering Mesopotamian cities. These centers of learning and religion had, for millennia, been making strides in the development of trade, diplomacy, and civic institutions, and Mesopotamian ideas were imposed upon or copied by surrounding settlements. But Elam also felt the impact of the more isolated highland peoples of the mountains to the north and east of Susa, who developed independently.

These diverse regions of lowland and mountain were inhabited from earliest times. By 7000 BC, village settlements had developed in both environments, with houses constructed of sun-baked bricks, some of which still bear the fingerprints of their makers. The villagers began to work with raw copper, first by hammering it, then by smelting the ore and casting the metal. And they learned to make pottery. At first their vessels were fashioned by hand and dried in the sun. Soon they discovered how to fire the clay in a kiln so the vessels would be harder and thus better able to hold liquids. The earliest decorated pottery had crude geometric designs incised or painted with liquid clay. Some scholars think these patterns echo the weaves of baskets that the pottery may have replaced as receptacles. The ceramicists later learned to shape their wares on a wheel and the decoration evolved into designs of astonishing sophistication. Such vessels have been found at a number of prehistoric sites, indicating the widespread diffusion of this pottery style and suggesting fruitful contact among the early inhabitants of the region.

Sometime around 4500 BC, a small settlement took shape on twin hills by the Shaur River. This was the start of Susa. On one hill, known as the acropolis, a brick platform, measuring approximately 262 feet long, 213 feet wide, and 31 feet high from its base, was put up. Probably towering nearly 60 feet over the surrounding plain, it

For almost 3,500 years, the roof of Tepti-ahar's baked-brick tomb (right) lay intact; but in 1965, roadwork unwittingly destroyed part of the structure. The 11-inch-tall clay head below, found in an artists' workshop strewn with shells, gold, sawed elephant bones, bronze tools, mosaic fragments, and bowls of dried pigments may be a funerary portrait of the king. The head had been modeled, polished, painted, and inlaid, and a hole had been drilled in the base, probably for mounting.

must have been visible for miles. There is evidence that a temple once stood upon it. But these structures were eventually destroyed, apparently by raiders. Around the time of this devastation, at least 1,000 men, women, and children were laid to rest at the base of the platform. Their remains were closely stacked, one on top of another, in a small area. Some bodies were missing parts. Many seemed to have been interred simultaneously.

Several archaeologists believe that these individuals died over a period of time and that their bodies were deposited first in a charnel house; then, when the flesh had rotted away, what was left of them was buried. But others think these people all died at the same time—perhaps in the sack of Susa, or in a famine or plague—and were consigned to a common grave by their survivors. Interred with some of the dead were such grave goods as axlike instruments of hammered copper; copper disks, some pierced, perhaps meant to be suspended from the neck; and clay bowls, cups, and beakers, with exquisitely painted decorations showing animals native to the area around Susa.

In the fourth millennium BC the great cities of Mesopotamia arose to the west of Susa. As these became rich and strong, they looked eastward to the treasures of Iran's mountains. Susa was the gateway to this wealth. At the beginning of the Proto-Elamite Period, around 3300 BC, the influence

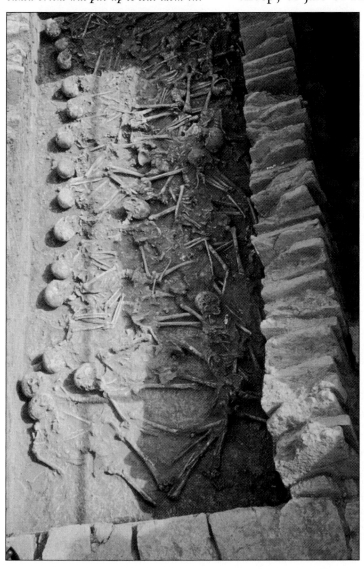

Skeletons form a neat line in a crudely built sepulcher adjacent to the tomb of Tepti-ahar. The Iranian archaeologist Ezat Negahban believes that they represent 14 members of the monarch's eternal guard, perhaps servants and wives sacrificed upon his death. Here the bodies were arranged in a row with faces to the north. Another nine skeletons lay helter-skelter atop the victims' leg bones. Unlike the king's tomb, which contained an additional 21 human sacrifices, this burial chamber had no door; once the bodies were placed inside, a rough barrier of baked bricks was put up to seal them in.

of the Mesopotamian city of Uruk was felt there. Because the few written records that exist from this time are still undeciphered, it is not clear whether people from Uruk actually lived in Susa, but the plain, mass-produced pottery of the period is very similar to that of Uruk. In addition, the Susians' engraved cylinder seals, stamped on clay to establish ownership, have similar images, carved in the same style as those found in Uruk.

With the growing exchange of ideas and trade, there emerged a whole new form of communication—writing. Early excavations at Susa yielded tiny clay and stone tokens. Their differing shapes are thought by archaeologists to indicate various items, such as grain, sheep, or jars of oil, which were being bartered. These were sometimes enclosed in hollow clay envelopes known as bullae, which were often impressed with markings identical to the tokens they concealed, thus showing at a glance the amount and type of the goods in a transaction. In cases where the necessary information was found on the bullae, the purpose of the tokens is thought to be to provide a means of quickly impressing this data on plain clay tablets. Out of the clay accounting tablets that evolved from this basic bookkeeping effort came a rudimentary cuneiform that included some characters from Uruk's own version of the wedge-shaped script, yet that overall was quite distinct from Uruk's. Scholars identify the language in which the early, still untranslated Susian inscriptions were written as Proto-Elamite, a precursor of Elamite. Surprisingly, this tongue does not fall into either the Indo-European or Semitic linguistic families, and has no known descendants.

While Proto-Elamite has not been deciphered, it crops up over a wide area as archaeological digs have shown, indicating a commercial network that included Susa and extended far into the Iranian highlands. Early tablets have been excavated in towns along the trade routes as far away as Godin Tepe, 170 miles to the north; Anshan, 320 miles to the southeast;

Shahr-i Sokhte, 450 miles east of Anshan, near Zahedan on the Afghanistan-Iran border; and Shahdad, at the edge of the Dasht-i-Lut desert, where more such writings have been found.

Anshan is perhaps the most interesting of these sites. As a center of power in its own right, it would share in the leadership of Elam, many of whose rulers styled themselves King of Anshan and Susa. (Later the Achaemenid monarchs would also use this prestigious title.) The location of Anshan remained unknown until 1970, when American archaeologist John Hansman, after examining various archaeological, textual, and linguistic references, proposed that the mounds at Tal-i-Malyan, a wide fertile valley in the Zagros Mountains, might conceal the ruins of the city. A University of Pennsylvania team, led by American archaeologist William Sumner, excavated there in the 1970s and unearthed portions of a Proto-Elamite settlement whose massive defense walls protected well-built rectangular houses of mud brick, and workshops complete with fireplaces and ovens. Bronzesmiths and potters had worked in the city, which had also housed merchants and farmers. Geometric designs in red, yellow, black, and white paint decorated the plastered walls of the rooms of buildings. Proof that this was indeed Anshan came when the archaeologists' trowels turned up bricks with the city's name clearly inscribed on them.

Anshan had been established around 3000 BC, perhaps by traders from Susa, who may have used it as a transfer point for shipping the copper and semiprecious stones of the eastern mountains to the population centers of Elam and Mesopotamia. Watered by the Kur River and surrounded by vineyards and fields of wheat, barley, grapes, and lentils, by stands of oak, juniper, poplar, almond, and pistachio, and by small satellite villages, Anshan grew swiftly. Within a few hundred years it was five times the size of Susa. Although its fortunes seem to have risen and fallen in the shadowy centuries that followed, its establishment was an early step in the alliance of principalities that would become Elam. Besides Susa and Anshan to the south and east, the Elamite kingdom would include Awan to the northwest and the province of Simash to the northeast, in the valleys of the Luristan Mountains.

In the following centuries, known as the Old Elamite Period (2600 to 1500 BC), Susa and Elam entered the historical archives of the Mesopotamians, the enemies of the Elamites. As writing developed in Mesopotamian cities, narratives began to be set down in clay,

For centuries, the ziggurat of King Untash Napirisha was known by the locals as Chogha Zanbil, or "basket mound," because it resembled an upside-down basket (below, right). Once excavation began on the 250-acre complex, hundreds of inscriptions proclaiming the king's name began coming to light. Also uncovered were hand-tooled, white and opaque blue or black glass rods (below) that, set diagonally into panels, decorated the ziggurat's wooden doors. Though no longer the capital of Elam, the city thrived until Ashurbanipal's savage attack left it in ruins.

including historical epics that claimed victories after bloody battles with Elam. Some of these accounts may be exaggerations or fictions, but they indicate that Elamite and Mesopotamian kings waged sporadic wars against one another over a long period. More convincing are the claims of a clay prism known as the Sumerian King List, first compiled around 2100 BC, long after most of the events noted had occurred. It outlines a history of repeated Mesopotamian triumphs over such various Elamite centers as Awan, Anshan, and Susa. Finally around 2300 BC, the armies of Mesopotamia, under the leadership of the city-state of Akkad, conquered Susa and absorbed it into a newly forming empire; this event was reflected in Susian sculptures, pottery, and records, inscribed in both the Akkadian and Elamite languages. The city seems to have become a staging point for the Akkadian kings' excursions farther east, a place where their charioteers and infantry could retire during the winter before resuming their offensives in the spring.

When the Akkadian empire collapsed about 2150 BC, King

Puzur-Inshushinak from the Elamite province of Awan, most likely in the mountains of Luristan north of Susa, retook Susa, but it was lost again to a new dynasty rising in the Mesopotamian city of Ur. Eventually Ur too declined, and again it was highlanders, this time from Shimashki, a province probably in the mountains northeast of Susa, who in 2004 BC took over the capital. According to later Mesopotamian lamentation poems, the rulers of Shimashki were strong enough to attack Ur itself and to lead its king into captivity. They also took away the statue of Ur's divine protector, the goddess Ningal, a sacrilege remembered long afterward in Mesopotamia.

The Shimashki gave way to another dynasty, about 1900 BC, known as the Sukkalmah. Votive and building inscriptions, as well as legal documents, offer some information about this relatively long-lived line. By tradition, Shimashki's rulers had come to use a title derived from the Sumerian language: Sukkal Mah, or Grand Regent. The Sukkal Mah governed with both a senior coregent (often his brother and heir, who bore the title of Sukkal of Elam and Shimashki) and a junior coregent, the Sukkal of Susa, who might be the son or nephew of the grand regent himself and was also in line to succeed him. This unusual system provided trained rulers; perhaps it also reduced dynastic intrigue.

Texts found at Susa indicate the growing power of the emergent Elamite state. Its agricultural wealth, derived from the irrigated farmland bordering Susa and the naturally watered high country, expanded. As records from Babylon to Syria attest, the Elamites were active in trade as well as in diplomacy and war. The triumvirate rule of the Sukkalmah dynasty continued, although no information survives about the last two centuries of their governance, except the names and titles of the rulers themselves. Then something dire seems to have happened. Archaeological surveys suggest that outlying villages near the cities were abandoned, and that the cities grew as the country people poured into them. Perhaps this was because of the decline in agricultural productivity around Susa and Anshan. This waning era would be followed by what scholars call the Middle Elamite Period (1500 to 1000 BC).

Despite the setback in its fortunes, Elam remained a force to be reckoned with. In the 15th century BC, a monarch named Tepti-ahar controlled the kingdom. Almost nothing was known about this monarch until the mid-1960s, when Iranian archaeologist Ezat Negahban began excavations at Tepti-ahar's majestic ceremonial city at Haft Tepe, about nine miles south of Susa. Negahban first saw Haft Tepe's 14 high mounds, "the majesty of the site in the light and shadow of the late-afternoon sun," as he put it, when he was a young student taking the train home to Ahwaz from the University of Tehran. Nineteen years later, in 1965, workers bulldozing the site for a sugarcane plantation noticed part of a baked-brick wall and reported it. Word reached the Archaeological Service of Iran, and before long, Negahban had assembled a team and begun the Haft Tepe excavations *(pages 20-21)*, which would continue until 1979, when the Iranian revolution brought work to a halt.

What Negahban found were the ruins of a series of magnificent buildings. Erected in the mid-15th century BC of brick held in place by gypsum mortar, the structures—which included halls, courts, kitchens, and workshops—were decorated with paint and plaster. Inside a walled temple-and-tomb complex more than 230 feet long and 98 feet wide was a huge central court that had a long portico at its northern end, behind which rose two temple halls, each leading to a tomb. In the court stood a stele inscribed in Akkadian, the language that, because of the influence of Mesopotamia and the general use of the Mesopotamian cuneiform script, had become the lingua franca of the Middle East. The monumental stone announced

Measuring almost two feet in length, this bronze tableau lay embedded in the wall of an Elamite tomb, three feet below the temple where the statue of Queen Napir-Asu (opposite) was found. A 12th-century inscription of an Elamite king identifies the scene as a sun ritual—the only three-dimensional example of worship in progress in the ancient Middle East. Here, two priests with shaved heads kneel, surrounded by miniature ziggurats, conical pillars, jars, basins, altars, and trees. Similar structures and basins were uncovered on the southeast, or sunrise, side of the ceremonial forecourt of Chogha Zanbil.

PRESERVATION'S GOAL: SAVE WHAT REMAINS OR SHOW WHAT ONCE WAS?

At the root of every archaeologist's search lies a passion to know what the found object looked like when new. This desire has often been keen enough to fuel efforts not only to preserve artifacts but to return them to their original appearance. The trio of terra-cotta panels below, 12th-century-BC decorations from the wall surrounding the Temple of Inshushinak at Susa, are examples. Each consists of 14 stacked bricks. Before putting the panels on display in 1930, restorers filled in chips, substituted plaster copies for missing bricks, and carefully painted each new piece—all in the hope of recapturing the impression the work made on viewers more than 3,000 years ago.

The panels constitute only a fraction of a collection of bricks from the wall taken to Paris after their discovery in Persia between 1912 and 1924. Most were placed untouched in storage, where they sat for six decades. During that time, the role of the art restorer changed dramatically. Humbled by the knowledge that future archaeological discoveries and technological advances might render the most enlightened of reconstructions obsolete, conservators today try to show the object as it really is.

So in 1990, when it was decided to reassemble three additional panels from the temple wall, the goal was not to improve them but simply to show what remained of them. "When we found fissures," the project director, Brigitte Bourgeois, explained, "flaws that were due to the manufacturing techniques of the ancients—their way of drying or baking the bricks, their way of mixing clay with chopped grass —then we left them as such." The result of conservators' efforts is seen at far right, below.

After more than six decades, the figures in this 1928 restoration of panels from the Temple of Inshushinak at Susa—a bull-man, a palm tree, and a goddess— appear almost new. Because the excavators were not able to locate the top two bricks of the goddess and her face was badly damaged, the restorers reworked her features and gave her a new headdress made of plaster (upper right).

Conservators use a microscope to identify minerals, traces of mortar, bitumen decoration, and other deposits on bricks that had been stored for more than 60 years. Such close examination also revealed the fingerprints of the artisans who first molded the bricks 3,000 years ago.

A sculptor fashions a new headdress for the goddess seen at left. Even after firing, the clay would have been easy to tell from the old. Yet in 1990, as shown at right, conservators of the similar, second work—unlike their 1928 counterparts—chose not to replace the missing part.

To accommodate future transport, as well as expected revisions and discoveries, the bricks in the 1991 reconstruction (right) were not fused permanently, but mounted on a metal frame. Conservators strengthened flaking bricks with synthetic resins that are easily soluble, and they did not rework or paint the blocks.

that in this place Tepti-ahar "built his tomb for himself and his favorite girl servant, and next to it he established a chapel and assigned to it priests, servants, and guards to serve and protect his tomb." The stele specified the amount of money allotted to pay for upkeep, regular ceremonies, and annual festivals.

And in fact when Negahban lifted the stone slabs covering a door in the eastern temple, he found a three-chambered tomb whose vaulted brick roof had survived for almost 3,500 years. Inside lay skeletons on brick platforms, seven on one, two on another, while a jumble of human bones formed a heap on the floor near the entry passage. It is likely that the second platform indeed held the remains of Tepti-ahar and his "favorite female servant"; the skeletons on the other platform may have been the remains of aides sacrificed to serve him in the afterlife. The pile of bones, Negahban thought, might have been those of sacrificed servants, or possibly wives. A tomb, adjacent to that of the king, was also crammed with skeletons (*page 21*).

Even in death Tepti-ahar may have had females to wait on him, according to Negahban. This suggestion is based on another of Tepti-ahar's documents, one whose provenance is uncertain. Its text reports that living women were locked into his vault at sundown to watch over him in the darkness. To prevent their stealing any of the tomb's now-vanished treasures, they had to wear tight dresses. That way, when they emerged each morning after their gruesome nightly stint, the temple priests could search them easily.

The many artifacts unearthed in the temples and workshops of Haft Tepe offer glimpses of the people who once lived and worked there. There are painted-clay statue heads with full, round faces, almond-shaped eyes, and braided hair, possibly portraits of the king and the ladies of the court, as well as small, nude, broad-thighed figures, sometimes identified as Ishtar, the Mesopotamian goddess of love and war. Thousands of clay tablets, with their clay envelopes still intact, proved upon examination to be letters and other texts dealing primarily with administrative matters. The tablets document

In 1904, French archaeologist Roland de Mecquenem discovered a 12th-century-BC cache of votive objects deposited in the sacred area of Susa's acropolis; among the objects were these two gold and silver figurines mounted on lumps of copper. Standing three inches high, they are almost identical representations of an Elamite king at worship. One hand is held forward in offering while the other holds a goat, probably intended for sacrifice. Another treasure from the cache is the 4½-inch-long lapis lazuli dove at right, studded with gold pegs.

an active Elamite bureaucracy that exchanged emissaries with Babylonia, and they reveal that relations between the two kingdoms were deteriorating during the reign of Tepti-ahar. Account tallies, school texts, and dictionaries also emerged from the earth to shed further light on daily life.

Among some of the most fascinating finds are interpretations of divination by examining sheeps' livers for omens, a widespread practice throughout the ancient Middle East. The meanings attributed to these signs suggest the nature of royal anxieties: "If on the lower part of the naplastu [a section of the liver] a piece is missing, the God Sin will help my army," says one line; if this should be the case on the right side, however, "problems will develop in my army." Worse, if the piece is missing in the upper part of the usurtu [another liver section], "fire will eat the main gate of my city."

For help in adversity, Elamites turned to a pantheon of deities. In fact, Negahban has suggested that their own name for their country, Hal-Tamti, may mean "Land of the Gods." Some of these divinities, such as Ishtar, had been imported from Mesopotamia; others were spirits of nature and vegetation, who manifested themselves throughout the ancient world. Among the latter was the ubiquitous Master of Animals, a human-shaped figure shown conquering demons and wild beasts. There were also deities peculiar to Elam, such as Inshushinak, the patron god of Susa who sat, as did other important Elamite divinities, on a serpent throne, pouring out precious water. Stone cylinder seals found at Haft Tepe bear engraved pictures of these gods, along with scenes of prayer, offering, and sacrifice.

Within a century of Tepti-ahar's reign, a new line of kings, known as the Igi-halkid family after an ancestor, were ruling Anshan and Susa. They and their successors, the Shutrukid dynasty, would build capitals and ceremonial centers rivaling those of Assyria and Babylon. The Igi-halkids' might would make them dangerous rivals; indeed, their depredations in Mesopotamia may in part explain the ferocity of Ashurbanipal's savage attack on Susa centuries later.

A king named Untash-Napirisha, fifth of the Igi-halkid line, who ruled Elam from about 1260 to 1235 BC, possessed the land, resources, and admin-

istration to begin major building and renovation projects at Susa as well as in towns and villages across the surrounding plain. His most remarkable project involved the construction of a new city 25 miles southeast of Susa. Untash-Napirisha may have intended it to replace Susa as both the religious and political center of Elam. The city, Al-Untash-Napirisha, was originally to have been dedicated solely to In-shushinak, patron god of Susa; but then, as building progressed, the dedication was extended to include Napirisha, the chief Elamite god. Some of the cuneiform inscriptions on the buildings are in Akkadian; others, however, are in Elamite. The ruins of Al-Untash-Napirisha lie at a place now called Chogha Zanbil, first spotted in the mid-1930s by people doing aerial surveys for an oil company. From 1936 to 1939, Roland de Mecquenem—who earlier had excavated at Susa—dug some exploratory trenches there. Major excavations of the 250-acre site were subsequently undertaken, between 1951 and 1962, by French archaeologist Roman Ghirshman.

Of the palaces, tombs, temples, and workshops that Ghirshman explored at Chogha Zanbil, the central and most impressive structure was a ziggurat *(page 23)* that must have rivaled those of Mesopotamia in its enormous size. Even in its ruined state it towered 82 feet above the plain; in Untash-Napirisha's day it is believed to have reared at least 170 feet.

The ziggurat was made up of a series of buildings, like enormous boxes nesting one inside the other. Piercing the 26-foot walls were monumental doors that opened onto vaulted stairways guarded by baked clay griffins and bulls. The stairs led in turn to offering chambers. Originally there were five stories; on the uppermost one a now-vanished temple had stood. Of these, only three survive.

Outside the ziggurat a walled precinct provided a setting for public ceremonies. People entered through three gates leading to a huge paved forecourt, lavishly decorated with bricks and tiles glazed in blue and green. Here, Ghirshman imagined, had been placed the thrones of Untash-Napirisha and his wife, Napir-Asu. When seated on them, the king and queen would have faced long tables where they could watch sacrifices and ritual cleansings conducted in the open air. Blood and libations drained from these altars into pits.

King Untash-Napirisha left behind evidence of how Elamite culture blended highland and lowland religious beliefs with those of Mesopotamia. He had an 8½-foot commemorative sandstone stele carved, which was first set up in the sacred precinct at Al-Untash-Napirisha, then transferred to Susa, where it was discovered in five fragments during early excavations from 1898 to 1909. On the stele, the king appears before a god to petition for "a dynasty of happiness." The deity, who sits on a throne that probably consisted of a folded serpent, has one human and one animal ear, perhaps an Elamite mark of divinity. He is Napirisha, usually depicted with flowing waters and snakes. Below is another image of the king, standing between the priestess U-Tik, perhaps his

Also found in many of the graves at Tepe Marlik were these highly stylized terra-cotta bull vessels. They were molded after the herds of humpbacked cattle that still graze in the region today. The heads serve as pouring spouts.

mother, and his queen, Napir-Asu. Underneath these figures are Mesopotamian mermaid goddesses. A similar cluster of deities appears on one of the most magnificent of the king's artifacts, a bronze and copper statue of the queen, about four feet high, discovered by Morgan at Susa *(page 24)*. Inscribed on her fringed skirt is a curse directed at anyone intending to do harm to her effigy. The curse invokes four divinities: Napirisha, whose name means the "Great God," and who was the chief Elamite deity; his consort Kiririsha, described as the "Lady of life, who has dominion over the sacred grove," and is the mother of the gods; Inshushinak, god of Susa; and Beltiya, meaning "My Lady" in Akkadian, a way of addressing the Mesopotamian goddess Ishtar.

Untash-Napirisha did not live to finish his city. Upon his death Susa regained its supremacy. Sacred but almost deserted, the fabulous Al-Untash-Napirisha stood for more than 600 years until it fell, like Susa, to Ashurbanipal's sweep through Elam.

Despite his desire to complete the city named after him, Untash-Napirisha did not neglect Susa. He and those who immediately succeeded him set in motion extravagant construction projects there for the honor of the gods and their own reigns, decorating the new buildings with treasures that had been seized during various conquests. Susa became a monument to the power of Elam, a city of palaces, temples, and sacred groves watered by an elaborate system of cisterns and canals.

Susa reached its apex under the Shutrukid kings, who built, rebuilt, and embellished its monuments with inscribed and decorated bricks glazed in blue, green, and white, and ornamented with colored knobs and wall plaques. Glazed bas reliefs depicted human figures and benevolent gods and goddesses wearing the horned crowns and animal heads of the region's long tradition. The Elamite style seems to emphasize both spaciousness and height: The houses of

Fanned by her attendant, an elegantly coiffed Elamite woman sits cross-legged on a lion-footed stool winding thread on a spindle while a meal of fish awaits on a table. This five-inch fragment of an eighth-century-BC relief was molded and carved from a mix of bitumen, ground calcite, and quartz. The Elamites also used bitumen, a naturally occurring mineral pitch, or asphalt, for vessels, sculpture, glue, caulking, and waterproofing.

Susa, for example, while laid out around courtyards according to the fashion of the Middle East, had unusually large audience halls or reception rooms, adorned at one or both ends with tall pilasters, columnlike structures that projected from the wall.

Susa's temples showed off the city's wealth. Among the objects found by early excavators in the ruins were gold and silver statues, small animal carvings of lapis lazuli and gold, and beads made of agate, carnelian, and gold filigree *(pages 28-29)*. Spoils of war from Mesopotamian cities such as Babylon, Sippar, Akkad, and Eshnunna further enriched Susa. One of the most outstanding was a seven-foot-high stele carved from black diorite and engraved with the legal code of Hammurabi, the king of Babylonia. The Elamites probably seized it from the Babylonian city of Sippar during an incursion into Mesopotamia and carted it home.

Aggressive kings known as the Shutrukids supplied much of the booty that adorned Susa. They reigned in the 12th century BC, an era that provided ample opportunities for burgeoning ambitions. With the Babylonian and Assyrian empires to the west and north weakened by internal strife and dynastic battles, the Shutrukids, as recorded in their own inscriptions as well as in Babylonian texts, raided, plundered, and destroyed. This brutal if lucrative activity reached its peak in mid-century, under a king named Shilhak-Inshushinak, who conquered central Mesopotamia and penetrated north across the Zagros Mountains into the heart of Assyria.

The Elamite incursions were bitterly remembered in the chronicles of towns taken and holy effigies purloined. Retaliation came at the end of the 12th century BC, in a strike at Elam by the Babylonian king, Nebuchadnezzar I. This onslaught seems to have been decisive, at least according to the Babylonian account, which stated bleakly, "The king of Elam disappeared permanently." What in fact occurred is a mystery; no recorded references to Elam over the next 300 years have so far come to light.

It is unlikely that Elam ceased to exist. The defeated Elamites may have suffered, as did the neighboring Mesopotamians, from crop failures and repeated famines, which in turn incited political unrest. Further complicating the picture would have been military threats from the north and west. In northern Mesopotamia, Assyria was gathering strength again, and at the northern end of the Zagros Mountains, the warrior-kings of Urartu were becoming more assertive. Farther east were the potentially dangerous Manneans, who lived in the area now known as Kurdistan. And entering the region for the first time were waves of the Indo-European peoples known as Aryans, who probably originated on the Steppe of southern Russia. These tribes may have appeared in Iran as early as 1400 BC, although some think they arrived 500 years later. Gradually they established strongholds. One group settled on the northwest Iranian plateau, another in the southwest. Among them were the ancestors of the Medes and the Persians.

Pressured from the north, west, and south and having lost control of their Mesopotamian borders and the territory surrounding Anshan, the Elamites, it is believed, retreated to the mountains around 1000 BC. Susa probably remained a political and ceremonial center, but when the story of the Elamites picks up again in written accounts of the ninth century BC, the Elamite kings and armies apparently have taken up residence in towns named Madaktu and Hidalu in the records.

During the period when the Elamites are missing from written accounts, other peoples come into focus, among them the originators of a burnished, gray pottery called Early Western Gray Ware, that began to spread throughout Iran beginning around 1400 BC. Some scholars have attributed the introduction of this ceramic to the Indo-European newcomers. Examples have generally been found in the cemeteries of settlements, including one at Tepe Marlik near the Caspian Sea. There, between 1961 and 1962, Negahban excavated 53 stone tombs, dating from about 1400 to 1000 BC, and retrieved large bronze animal statuettes, bronze weapons, gold jewelry, cylinder seals, glass beakers, and gold, silver, and bronze vessels.

Other citadels have also yielded splendid treasures. In 1947 local shepherds climbing a hill in Kurdistan, once the land of the Manneans, stumbled upon a few gold artifacts and in their efforts to sell them attracted the attention of nearby villagers and dealers in antiquities. The result was the marketing of a multitude of objects allegedly taken from this remote site, now displayed in museums around the world. One of the choicest is a gold breastplate decorated with mythical animals and winged creatures, partly human, now in the Archaeological Museum of Tehran *(pages 50-51)*. The French archaeologist Andre Godard, who studied the artifacts, believes that the breastplate dates to the end of the eighth century BC, when

JOY AND DREAD AT HASANLU

It is an accepted feature of archaeology that little, if any, of the emotion felt in the field ever makes its way into the final report. Yet to judge from the experiences of American and Iranian excavators at Hasanlu, an 80-foot-high mound near Lake Urmia in northwestern Iran, digging at a site can evoke a wide range of feelings.

The archaeologists started work in 1957 under the direction of the University of Pennsylvania archaeologist Robert H. Dyson Jr. They soon came across what he called the "discovery of a lifetime." Under a layer of charred debris in the ru-

ins of one of five monumental buildings on the site, a worker found human bones. As Dyson and his assistants brushed away the dirt, the glint of metal caught their eye. "Thinking it was a bracelet," Dyson recalled, "I brushed some more. Our eyes got bigger and bigger as the sliver became a strip, and then a sheet, and then a golden bowl." Spirits were so high after the 1958 discovery that Dyson raised the crumpled vessel overhead in triumph *(left)*. Then he and his team washed the bowl, filled it with wine, and drank a toast to their good fortune.

Further digging revealed weapons and silver, gold, and ivory artifacts, indications that the fire that consumed Hasanlu spread too quickly for the attackers to loot it. But the spadework also brought to light evidence of a disaster: 246 skeletons of men, women, children, and infants, more than half of whom had apparently been crushed under collapsing walls

and roofs. Excavators found the remaining bodies in open areas. Possessing gruesome head wounds or severed limbs, they apparently had been victims of a bloody slaughter. "Not a few archaeologists who excavated at the site," a scholar wrote, "were emotionally affected by the carnage and the human suffering that had taken place."

The skeleton of a man, one of hundreds found at Hasanlu, lies facedown where he fell in a battle fought about 800 BC. The broken sword in his right hand identifies him as a warrior, but experts cannot say if he was a defender or an attacker.

The gold cup below was so prized that at least three people at ancient Hasanlu died protecting—or stealing—it. The scene shows a storm god goading a bull spewing water onto the land and a boxer fighting a monster.

the Mannean stronghold was ravaged by Assyrian king Sargon II, who turned upon his erstwhile Mannean allies and destroyed their cities. Others think the city fell to marauding Scythian horsemen in the seventh century BC.

The most impressive of these Gray Ware sites, Hasanlu, sat on the trade routes that linked Assyria, Urartu, and the Mannean lands. American archaeologist Robert H. Dyson Jr. began excavations at Hasanlu in 1957 *(pages 34-35)*, exposing what was left of its fortifications and columned halls with spiral staircases, believed by some scholars to be temples. From its remains he reconstructed the city's fiery end in about 800 BC, when Urartu sacked the city.

The great enemies of Urartu, as of most Middle Eastern kingdoms at this time, were Assyria's warrior-kings, who left their bloody imprints on the history of every nation in the Middle East. One of the earliest mentions of the Elamite kingdom, after the 300-year silence, is a report in a Babylonian chronicle noting that in 814 BC, Elamite troops aided the Babylonians in a battle against the Assyrians. The reappearance of Elam in records occurs during the Neo-Elamite Period (743 to 500 BC), and is further attested to in Babylonian chronicles, Assyrian inscriptions, and ancient correspondence.

It was an age of constant warfare, with Assyria almost always the victor. In 689 BC, Babylon fell to Assyrian king Sennacherib, who, after plundering the city and slaughtering many of its citizens, stacked the corpses in the streets and burned the city to the ground. By 653, Sennacherib's grandson Ashurbanipal had killed Elam's leaders and placed client kings in the towns of Hidalu and Madaktu. Elam was then torn by factions and revolts against its discredited monarchy. Then in 647 came the infamous Assyrian invasion, when Ashurbanipal chased Humban-Haltash III, the reigning king, into the eastern mountains, sacked Susa, and pillaged the countryside.

But the Assyrian yoke would be thrown off in 612 BC by an alliance of the Babylonians and the Medes. In the succeeding century of Neo-Babylonian hegemony the fragmented remains of Elam would take on new life and its capital new splendor. The stage was set for the flowering of Persia.

FLIGHT PATHS TO DISCOVERY

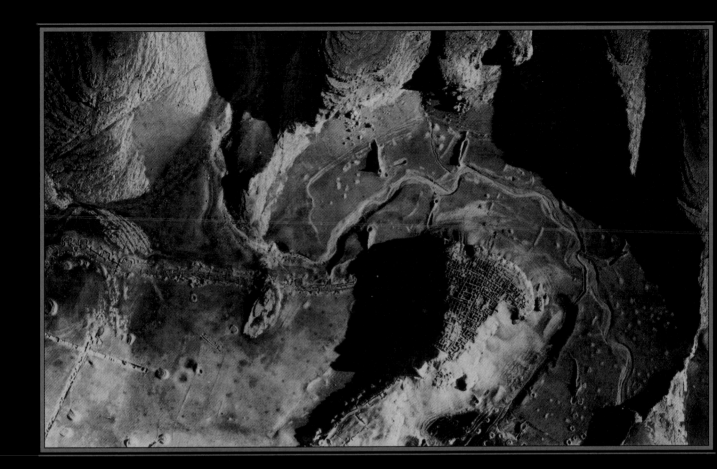

In 1935 Mary Helen Schmidt, a wealthy American, gave a gift to her German-born husband, archaeologist Erich F. Schmidt, director of three Iranian expeditions. It was a Waco biplane, equipped with a 220-horsepower engine. Dubbed *Friend of Iran*, the craft was soon crisscrossing the country, as it would until 1938. Although a few sites in other nations had been photographed from the air, Schmidt's plane would lead—as Mrs. Schmidt had hoped—to the first large-scale, carefully planned aerial survey of ancient ruins.

The regions under Schmidt's direction—Persepolis in the south, Rayy near Tehran in the north, and Luristan in the Zagros Mountains—ranked at the top of his aerial agenda. He made hundreds of dazzling, panoramic overviews with his camera, like the shot above of Qasr-i-Abu, a seventh-century-AD Sassanian citadel in southern Iran. Such images helped pinpoint areas for exploration. Commuting time was saved by flying between the three areas, and en route Schmidt

and his colleagues learned, in his words, to "see faster."

Overhead photography was a challenge. Shooting through a hole in the bottom of the plane proved inadequate until a suspension mechanism was attached. It held the camera and a telescope that showed the landscape in crisp detail. Thanks to built-in leveling devices, both adjusted to a horizontal position that allowed the photographer to get the picture he wanted. While vertical views were essential for mapping, oblique photos proved more useful for assessing the relative heights of buildings, columns, and walls. The team also found that the spring and the moments after sunrise offered the best opportunities; the features of the terrain were more sharply defined then than at other times.

Most important, the team was able to chart unknown territory for future excavation. It took a mere 13 hours of flying to cover more than 400 ancient sites on the plain of Persepolis, a task that, Schmidt figured would have taken years on the ground.

Overhead photographs of Persepolis, such as this one, reveal the city's layout. The lower left quadrant shows Schmidt's 1935-1936 excavation of Darius I's capital. Fortifying walls enclose the "crumbs," as Schmidt put it, of magnificent palaces set aflame by Alexander the Great in 330 BC. Columns and ramparts, shot in early-morning light, cast long shadows that indicate their relative heights. The largest squarelike structure is the huge Apadana, or audience hall. The smaller one behind it is the Hall of 100 Columns, and the long, rectangular, roofed building to its side is dig headquarters. The rows of ringed dots to the right of the city are wells of a contemporary irrigation system. Similar vertical shots of other archaeological sites made direct mapping of them by Schmidt and team quick, easy, and accurate.

Early on the morning of July 27, 1937, Schmidt and his flight crew, which always included his wife, circled the oval fortress of Takht-i-Suleiman, or "Throne of Solomon" (below), snapping a photo whenever the sun pierced the cloud cover. Set on a natural rise amid a mosaic of cultivated fields 250 miles west of Tehran, the citadel was occupied from the Parthian to the Mongol era, a span of some 1,300 years. Each Sassanian ruler, according to legend, journeyed there to humble himself at the sacred altar of the fire god before ascending the throne. The remains of the altar lie at the center of a group of rectangular buildings, to the left of the deep lake. The uneven surface of the citadel is made up of the ruins of many small dwellings, believed to have housed soldiers and priests.

I AM CYRUS,
KING
OF
THE WORLD

Crossing the Murghab plain in 330 BC, an army threaded its way along the flank of a steep, wooded gorge above the stream known today as the Pulvar. The troops were under the command of the young Macedonian conqueror Alexander, who was pressing eastward, dreaming of empire. They entered a broad, grassy valley. Half-hidden by a cluster of gnarled trees, they caught a glimpse of a structure that, for a solemn moment, would bring their impatient general to a halt.

Alexander had arrived at the site of the Persian capital of Pasargadae and had come upon the tomb of an earlier, celebrated world conqueror, the Persian king Cyrus II, known as Cyrus the Great. In his day, Cyrus had founded an empire of unprecedented size and power. Because Alexander hoped to surpass the Persian monarch's achievements, he felt compelled to pause here and pay homage to his acclaimed predecessor.

One of Alexander's comrades in arms, Aristobulus, gave an account of their visit to the tomb, which later found its way into the writings of the first-century-BC Greek geographer Strabo. It was "a tower of no great size," Aristobulus reported, "concealed beneath the thicket of trees, in its lower parts massive, but its upper parts having a roof and shrine with a very narrow entrance." The Macedonians cautiously entered the building, all of 200 years old at the time. They

A gold plaque of the fifth or fourth century BC shows a man in Median dress carrying a bundle of sticks, perhaps for use in a ritual. Before being conquered by the Persians, the Medes were the ruling force, with a sphere of influence that may have extended from eastern Turkey to northern Afghanistan.

found themselves in the royal burial chamber, where according to Aristobulus, they beheld "a golden couch and table with drinking cups, and a golden coffin."

There was also an inscription, cited "from memory," by Aristobulus: "Oh man, I am Cyrus, who founded the empire of the Persians and was king of Asia. Grudge me not therefore this monument." The Greek historian Plutarch, writing Alexander's biography in the late first century AD, reported that as a mark of respect Alexander had ordered a Greek translation of the Persian text to be carved alongside it. Plutarch also offered a somewhat more melodramatic version of Cyrus's original text, which may have been taken from a source other than Aristobulus or embellished in its passage through the intervening centuries: "Oh man, whosoever thou art and from whencesoever thou comest (for that thou wilt come I know), I am Cyrus, who founded the empire of the Persians. Grudge me not, therefore, this little earth that covers my body."

The inscriptions vanished; indeed, some scholars doubt that they existed. But the tomb remained to intrigue foreign travelers of a much later age. An early-19th-century visitor, Claudius James Rich, confessed that "the very venerable appearance of the ruin instantly awed me. I found that I had no right conception of it. I sat for nearly an hour on the steps, contemplating it until the moon rose on it, and I began to think that this in reality must be the tomb of the best, the most illustrious, and the most interesting of oriental sovereigns."

None of these superlatives capture the personality or competence of Cyrus, a leader of remarkable intelligence, strength, and vision. He was a dynamic force in a turbulent age, the middle of the first millennium BC. He guided the transformation of the Persians from an obscure ethnic group into the masters of an empire that would extend from the Indian Ocean to the Aegean Sea and rule the lives of such diverse, distant peoples as the Steppe dwellers of Central Asia, Nile fishermen, nomads of the Libyan desert, Hebrews, Greeks, Mesopotamians, and the mountain tribes of what is now Afghanistan. Never before had a single, centralized authority united a population so numerous, varied, and far-flung.

Cyrus and his successors, Cambyses II and Darius I, accomplished this rise to power in little more than a half-century. The dynasty that Cyrus founded became known as the Achaemenid after an

Constructed out of large blocks of stone, the austere tomb of the Persian king Cyrus the Great rears more than 35 feet high on the windswept Murghab plain. Cultural influences evident in the architecture of the monument—from Mesopotamian stepped ziggurats to Anatolian tombs—suggest that Cyrus was eager to adopt ideas from the variety of peoples who inhabited his vast empire.

alleged ancestor, Achaemenes. The Achaemenid empire survived for some 200 years, and its political, social, and cultural imprints were embedded in the centuries of imperial rule that followed under other dynasties. The Achaemenids' methods of conquest and government served as an example to the later empire builders of Greece and Rome; their spiritual beliefs influenced the shape of other religions; their inscriptions, monuments, and ruined cities enlightened historians and challenged archaeologists.

An archaeological record of the Achaemenids' ascendancy and triumph has been assembled from excavations carried out at splendid royal capitals and humbler settlements. These have yielded numerous messsages, structures, sculptures, and artifacts that answer many questions about the civilization that created them, but give rise to others. At the base of the archaeological record are the works of ancient chroniclers. Their reports owe their existence, in part, to the cultural and political ferment of the times. As armies tramped east or west between the Middle East and Europe, so too did diplomats, merchants, physicians, colonists, soldiers of fortune, and other travelers. The vivid accounts of these observers were given circulation, sometimes in distorted form, and often picked up and passed on by such noted Greek authors as Xenophon, Herodotus, and Strabo. There is also the testimony of the compilers of the Old Testament, the Judeans, whose forebears were caught up in the whirlwind of Middle Eastern politics. Other kingdoms under Persian rule provided evidence of Achaemenid greatness in letters, treaties, and military annals. Joining the texts of these vassal peoples are the words of the Achaemenid kings themselves, eager to set down for posterity their own versions of events. It is hardly surprising then that the reports provided by these different sources are, at times, contradictory.

The records do agree, however, that when Cyrus the Great came to manhood, the Middle East was ripe for political restructuring. For some 2,000 years, the region had been influenced or dominated by Egypt and Mesopotamia. By the early first millennium BC, however, previously unknown peoples were rising, among them the Medes of the Iranian Plateau. By the late seventh century BC, the Medes had made the transition from a group of different tribes to a single political entity. They became allies of Babylon in a fierce military offensive against Assyria that brought about a dramatic change in the Middle Eastern power structure.

Evidence of Median importance in that alliance appeared some 26 centuries later in 1955, when a team from the British School of Archaeology in Iraq, led by Max Mallowan, was sifting through ruins in the Assyrian capital of Nimrud. The archaeologists were clearing debris from a throne room razed by Median invaders in 612 BC. There they found some 350 fragments of baked-clay tablets bearing cuneiform inscriptions. Piecing together this massive jigsaw puzzle, Barbara Parker, a member of the team, identified the tablets as the official records of treaties made in 672 BC between the Assyrian king Esarhaddon and the chieftains of many different tribes or cities, including those of the Medes.

The mingling of peoples and cultures that helped shape the history of the ancient Middle East often had fertile effect on its art as well. A melding of styles, this gold pectoral, which dates between the eighth and seventh centuries BC and is more than one foot across, was apparently among treasures buried for safekeeping in a bronze tub at Ziwiye, site of a ruined fortress in northwest Iran. No one knows whether this hoard of gold, silver, and ivory—found in 1947 by a shepherd boy and dispersed before it could be properly studied— was hidden by a defender of the

fortress or by a plunderer who intended to come back for it. Nor can anyone say whether the fortress was built by the Assyrians or by their rivals, the Manneans. But the execution and iconography of the pectoral suggests that its maker had ecclectic taste and that the fortress's inhabitants were more cosmopolitan than might have been imagined.

The piece is divided into two bands, with ribbonlike trees of Urartian design at its center. In each of the upper corners crouches a beast that indicates the influence of the Scythians, nomadic horsemen who may have been responsible for the fort's destruction. In both panels, various winged beasts echo the art of lands as far-flung as Assyria, Syria, Phoenicia, and perhaps Greece.

The documents asserted the loyalty of all these leaders to Esarhaddon, whom they affirmed as their supreme overlord. They agreed to stringent terms of obedience to his designated heir: "You will protect Ashurbanipal, the crown prince. You will not sin against him; you will not bring your hand against him with evil intent. You will not revolt. You will not oust him from the kingship of Assyria by helping one of his brothers, older or younger, to seize the throne of Assyria in his stead." The conditions of the contract ran on at length, ending with the injunction that "whoever changes, neglects, or transgresses the oaths of this tablet, or erases it . . . may Ninurta, chief of the gods, fell you with his swift arrow; may he fill the plain with your corpses; may he feed your flesh to the eagle and jackal."

Obviously the Medes, who subsequently burst into the inner sanctum and sacked the palace, were undaunted by these threats. The deliberately shattered tablets, their pieces heaped around the violated throne dais, represented a new political fact: Assyrian kings, after more than 300 years of supremacy, were no longer masters of the Medes or other peoples of western Iran. Four powers now dominated the Middle East: Egypt's pharaohs; the Babylonians, commanding the lands between the Tigris and Euphrates Rivers, and soon to extend their influence westward through Syria and Palestine to the Mediterranean Sea; the Lydians in western Anatolia; and the Medes, who had taken over the northern part of the Assyrian empire, including eastern Anatolia and northwestern Persia.

The Medes shared a similar background with the Persians, who did not, at this time, assert themselves beyond their own small settlements. Both were Indo-European peoples, speaking closely related languages, who upon emerging from Central Asia had settled in the Zagros Mountains of western Persia. They were first mentioned in the military annals of ninth-century-BC Assyrian kings, and until Assyria's eclipse, both Medes and Persians continued to appear in these documents as holders of lands through which the imperial army passed or as tribute-paying vassals.

In 1965, for instance, archaeologists Louis Levine and T. Cuyler Young, both of the Royal Ontario Museum in Toronto, Canada, were excavating a Median site at Godin Tepe in central Iran. They heard rumors from local people of an ancient inscription in a nearby village. Following up these leads, they discovered the first Assyrian

monument yet found on the Iranian Plateau, a stele erected by the late-eighth-century-BC monarch Sargon II. The inscription provided a wealth of previously unknown details about Sargon's military movements through Median territories in his six campaigns to extend and hold the empire's eastern borders.

Texts such as those on Sargon's stele provide much of what is known today about the Medes. Unfortunately, the Median archives have not yet been found, although they may lie buried at the site of the Medes' ancient capital of Hagmatana, known to the ancient Greeks as Ecbatana. Whatever remains of Ecbatana lies today beneath the modern Iranian city of Hamadan, 25 miles east of Godin Tepe.

In Ecbatana, in the shadow of the imposing snow-capped heights of Mount Alvand, the Medes built a royal fortress. This edifice was remarkable, according to Herodotus, ringed with seven concentric walls, each apparently painted a different color. At its center, closest to the heart of Median power, stood the two innermost fortification walls, supposedly covered in plates of silver and gold.

Although the Ecbatana of the Medes may be inaccessible for immediate study, two other Median sites—in addition to Godin Tepe—have been explored; these are Tepe Baba Jan and Tepe Nush-i Jan, near Hamadan. The first mound, Tepe Baba Jan, excavated by British archaeologist Clare Goff in the late 1960s, offers a tantalizing glimpse of a grand building, which Goff considered Median but which, according to other scholarly opinion, may be earlier. The

Built some 100 feet above an ancient riverbed, this 2,700-year-old fortification at Godin Tepe was used by the Medes, perhaps under governance of a local khan, or prince, during the seventh century BC. For reasons unknown, the site was abandoned in the next century and was then taken over by squatters.

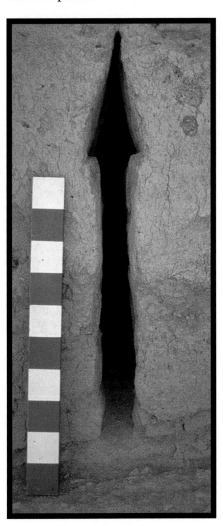

Although the Medes at Godin Tepe originally seemed concerned with defense, improving the fortress here with ramparts and arsenals, they eventually ceased to maintain it. Arrow slots, like the one shown below with an archaeologist's measuring rod, filled up with debris and were even plastered over.

structure might have been a temple, a throne room, or perhaps the luxurious residence of royal or upper-class Medes. Its centerpiece seems to have been a richly decorated chamber, painted in red and white and adorned with red-and-white patterned tiles.

The decade-long dig at Tepe Nush-i Jan, beginning in 1967, was the work of British archaeologists David Stronach and Michael Roaf, sponsored by the British Institute of Persian Studies. There they uncovered a fortified Median settlement that resembled those depicted on the sculpted stone walls of Assyrian palaces.

A mystery lay at the heart of Tepe Nush-i Jan: In the late seventh century BC, part of the site, including a religious sanctuary with an altar, was carefully sealed. The people who carried out this work were meticulous in their attempt to cover up the structure in a way that would not only hide it but protect it from damage. They filled it with shale, then heaped upon it alternate layers of packed shale chips and mud bricks and surrounded it by massive brickwork barriers *(page 56)*. The reasons for their effort are unknown.

In 590 BC, the Medes, by this time an established and centralized kingdom, began to expand their dominions. Under their monarch Cyaxares, they marched into Anatolia in an effort to wrest it from the Lydians. This was a land worth fighting for: Its earth was veined with gold mines, and sometime in the late seventh or early sixth century BC, its inhabitants had invented coinage as a means of facilitating its proliferating trade. Herodotus reports that the Medes and Lydians battled incessantly for five years, until both sides were stopped in their tracks by a sudden, total, and terrifying eclipse of the sun on May 28 in 585 BC.

The gods, in the view of both warring parties, obviously wanted hostilities to end. So to seal the peace, the king of Lydia, Alyattes, gave his daughter's hand in marriage to Astyages, heir to the Median throne. Alyattes died soon thereafter, and he was buried with all the splendor due to the region's richest king. His tumulus still stands in western Turkey, just north of the ruins of the old city of Sardis. Emptied long ago of its treasure, it is believed to be the largest tepe that survives from ancient times.

Alyattes' son and heir, Croesus, whose name is still a byword for virtually unlimited wealth, ascended the throne of Lydia. Still bearing a grudge against the Medes, Croesus bided his time. It was some 35 years after the momentous solar eclipse, in 550 BC, when he received the news that his old enemies were in trouble. A Persian king named Cyrus, he was told, had deposed King Astyages, plundered the monarch's treasury at Ecbatana, and had appropriated the whole of the Median empire. Croesus saw his opportunity. He mustered his armies and marched eastward, hoping to expand his own territory by filching some of the former lands of the Medes. It was a blunder that would cost him his entire domain.

Croesus had undoubtedly failed to take the measure of his opponent, Cyrus II, a ruler who would eventually achieve such stature that the details of his life would become clouded by an accumulation of folklore. The Persian king's birth, believed to have occurred in 598 BC, is overlaid with myth. Cyrus was said to have been abandoned in infancy because of an evil omen and to have been nursed by a dog. Like the biblical hero Moses, he was then supposed to have been rescued from near-certain death and reared by adoptive parents, in order to fulfill his destiny. Herodotus recounts some of this lore, but both he and Xenophon, a Greek soldier and historian writing in the fourth century BC, provide a less fantastic version of Cyrus's beginnings: They assert that his father was a Persian prince, his mother the daughter of Astyages, the last ruler of the Medes.

Whether or not Cyrus was, in fact, Astyages' grandson, virtually all chroniclers of the age agree that he was the man who defeated and deposed the old Median king in 550 BC. Some contemporary reports suggest that Cyrus was originally a vassal of Astyages' who rose up and rebelled against his Median overlord; others say that he was an ambitious outsider casting a covetous eye on his neighbor's dominions. He had been a ruler of the Persians for eight years before challenging the Medes.

A curious inscription by the mystically inclined Nabonidus, king of Babylon, relates how his victory over the Medes was foretold by his god, Marduk, chief deity of Babylon, in a dream: Nabonidus complained to Marduk that the Medes had occupied an ancient temple, which the deity had specifically commanded Nabonidus to rebuild. Marduk then reassured the Babylonian king with a prophesy of doom for the Medes. "They, their country, and all the kings, their allies, no longer exist," Marduk supposedly said; he then went on to predict that Cyrus would "expel them." Shortly afterward Nabonidus learned of the Medes' undoing at the hands of the Per-

The chamber above at Tepe Baba Jan in eastern Luristan reflects a rare usage of bright color in early-first-millennium local architecture. More than 170 painted clay tiles, decorated with geometric patterns (left), were discovered lying on the floor of the chamber, where they may have ended up after falling from the ceiling when a fire ravaged the site.

sians and declared in an inscription on a stele that the surprise victory of Cyrus "with his small army" was really the work of Babylon's avenging god.

Ironically, Cyrus would later use his reputation as an agent of Marduk against Nabonidus himself. He enjoyed a considerable amount of earthly support as well, says Herodotus. A malcontent Median general, sent by Astyages to put down the upstart Persian, had old scores to settle against his own monarch. So the general promptly defected, along with his entire army, and helped Cyrus defeat Astyages to become king of both the Medes and the Persians.

A work called *The Education of Cyrus*, written by Xenophon, probably includes genuine biography as well as a substantial amount of fiction. Xenophon is likely to have drawn many details from Persian tradition in his portrayal of Cyrus as a brilliant military commander, decisive and imaginative in his tactics, and respected by his men. According to Xenophon, Cyrus was a stickler for military discipline but keen to build morale, scrupulously fair, and democratic in the distribution of rewards. He was lavish in his hospitality, inviting low-ranking soldiers as well as senior officers to dine in his tent. "In every case," Xenophon reports, "there was no distinction whatever between the meats for himself and for his guests." Further, he always insisted that military servants share in everything given the men they served. Those who did such service for the army, he believed, were as much to be honored as heralds or ambassadors since they were required to be "loyal and intelligent, alive to all a soldier's needs, active, swift, unhesitating, and withal, cool and imperturbable."

Cyrus's empire building continued when he defeated Croesus in 546 BC. The gold and silver of Lydia, together with the rich spoils of the Greek merchant cities of Ionia, formerly under Lydian control, would fund the march of Persian armies. There were reasons for expansion besides personal ambition. From the north and east, beyond present-day Afghanistan, nomadic tribes menaced the Iranian Plateau. For the security of the Persian heartland, Cyrus needed to extend his political control and military presence as far into Central Asia as possible. Little archaeological evidence has been found of his eastward movements, but the name Cyropolis, given to a settlement on the Jaxartes River east of the Aral Sea in present-day Kazakhstan, is believed to mark the site of one of Cyrus's frontier posts.

To the west of Persia lay the Mediterranean seaports, where the wealth of all the ancient world changed hands; to the south, along

The remains of the Median site known as Tepe Nush-i Jan sprawl atop a shale outcrop that rises 121 feet above the Jowkar plain in northern Iran, 37 miles south of the as-yet-unexcavated Median capital of Ecbatana at Hamadan. Archaeologists have uncovered several structures at Nush-i Jan—including a fort and two temples—built by the Medes around 750 BC. The buildings were deserted in the sixth century BC, and as at Godin Tepe, the site was occupied by squatters.

Excavations in 1970 at Nush-i Jan by British archaeologist David Stronach revealed a temple with a fire altar at the bottom of this eighth-century-BC tower, which had been carefully filled with shale and then abandoned. The use of fire here, apparently during rites, may foreshadow its broader application in the Zoroastrian religion, which was to gain large numbers of Persian adherents in the next centuries.

the shores of the Persian Gulf, were lands grown rich from the passage of India-bound caravans. It was in this southern region, according to Strabo, that Cyrus built a palace "on the coast near Taoke, as it is called." In 1971, Iranian archaeologist Ali Akbar Safaraz excavated in an area near Borazjan, where Achaemenid objects had been found close to a road some 18 miles from the Persian Gulf shore. In the ruins of a building, he unearthed two rows of elegantly carved column bases, in a style dating from Cyrus's reign, and concluded that he had found the royal residence of which Strabo had spoken.

The jewel of cities was the wealthy Babylon. Those who tell the tale of its conquest by Cyrus in 539 BC agree that it was formidably well defended. Herodotus, who visited the site, reports that its first line of defense was a moat surrounding a 56-mile circuit of brickwork ramparts 300 feet high. These walls were so thick that, at the top, they supported a roadway wide enough to accommodate a four-horse chariot. Within this perimeter reared a second wall, equally stout in its construction. One hundred bronze gates, each heavily and permanently guarded, provided access to the city.

Its defenders asserted that Babylon was virtually siege-proof. There was no lack of fresh water, since the Euphrates River ran through town, and according to Xenophon, the granaries held enough food to sustain the inhabitants for more than 20 years.

If brute force could not bring Babylon down, Cyrus had other methods. Some sources claim that Cyrus had prepared the ground for his invasion over several years, by supporting political and religious malcontents within Babylon and its dominions. He also orchestrated one of history's earliest propaganda campaigns—against the weak king Nabonidus and Belshazzar, his even more unpopular son. Nabonidus had alienated his people by acts of religious heresy: most important, by absenting himself from the capital for a decade, staying away even during the most sacred festivals, when the future prosperity of the realm depended on the presence in Babylon of its ruler, who was required to perform certain rites. He had also done little to repair relations with his subject peoples, such as the Jews, who had been forcibly transplanted from Jerusalem to Babylon by his predecessor, Nebuchadnezzar II, and remained there as exiles under Nabonidus.

A hoard of silver lies exposed to daylight some 2,000 years after being packed into a bronze bowl (below) and buried under the floor in a fort at Tepe Nush-i Jan. The spirals, dating to the third millennium BC, were among more than 100 items in the bowl. The pieces may have been meant for use as a means of payment in commercial transactions.

The main thrust of Cyrus's public-relations offensive was that Nabonidus had offended many gods and peoples, and that Cyrus was divinely appointed to bring him down. The Persian king had promised to respect the gods of Babylon, and in his incursions into other Mesopotamian cities before he reached the capital, he was as good as his word. A Babylonian chronicle reports that there were no interruptions of religious rites as his army marched through the land between the Tigris and Euphrates Rivers.

By October 12 the Persians had reached Babylon. Both Herodotus and Xenophon indicate that on that date a religious festival occupied the attention of the city's inhabitants. Meanwhile, Gobryas, the rebellious governor of Gutium, a province east of the Tigris River, was directing the would-be invaders in a strategy that had been conceived by Cyrus: Under cover of darkness and the noise of thousands of not-quite-sober citizens enjoying themselves in honor of their gods, Gobryas's soldiers reached the city walls and quietly began digging a huge trench to divert the Euphrates from its course.

Neither Herodotus nor Xenophon reports the reaction of guards who may have been posted at the water gates when the stream bubbled away before their eyes, to be replaced by several columns of marching soldiers. Herodotus notes, however, that "owing to the size of the place, the inhabitants of the central parts, long after the outer portions of the town were taken, knew nothing of what had changed." Apparently they "continued dancing and reveling until they learned the news the hard way."

Whatever the fact of this story, most historians think that Cyrus entered Babylon peacefully and was welcomed by its population. The Persian king's own verdict on his victory survives on a clay cylinder found by archaeologists in Babylon in 1879, at the site of the Temple of Marduk: "I en-

Discovered in western Turkey, these magnificent silver bowls and pitchers from the mid-sixth century BC lend credence to the saying "rich as Croesus." About this time, Cyrus the Great focused his ambition on the west, defeating the wealthy Lydian king in Sardis and looting Croesus's treasuries. The Persians used the precious objects to finance military campaigns.

tered Babylon as a friend and I established the seat of the government in the palace of the ruler under jubilation and rejoicing. My numerous troops walked around in Babylon in peace, I did not allow anybody to terrorize." He proclaimed himself the choice of Babylon's chief god, Marduk, who "scanned all the countries searching for a righteous ruler" and of course found one: "He pronounced the name of Cyrus, King of Anshan."

Cyrus II also notes on the cylinder some of his civic reforms, which included abolishing the highly unpopular forced-labor plan of the previous regime. The public works program that he introduced was the kind that wins votes for today's politicians: "I brought relief to their dilapidated housing, putting an end to their complaints."

The inscription offers as expansive a definition of his realm as he could conceivably imagine: "I am Cyrus, king of the world, great king, legitimate king, king of Babylon, king of Sumer and Akkad, king of the four quarters of the earth." Such boasts are seldom taken at face value by archaeologists, but in this case they were not far out of line with reality, for Cyrus's conquest of Babylon gave him lordship over an empire of subject kings. They ranged from palace-dwelling monarchs to nomadic chieftains, each apparently ready to swear loyalty to the Achaemenid vanquisher. "All the kings of the entire world," Cyrus tells us, "from the Upper to the Lower Sea, those who are seated in throne rooms, those who live in other sorts of buildings, as well as all the kings of the West living in tents, brought their heavy tributes and kissed my feet in Babylon."

While his own scribes can be expected to extol him, texts from many different sources also give the new ruler a remarkably good reputation. The Jews, delighted when Cyrus released them from Babylonian exile and allowed them to return to their homeland and rebuild the Temple, praised him as the "Lord's anointed." Although strictly monotheistic, they nevertheless concurred with Cyrus's view of himself as divinely favored. In the book of Isaiah, the prophet announces: "Thus says God to his anointed, to Cyrus whom he grasps by his right hand, that he might subdue nations before him, and ungird the loins of kings, to open doors before him, that gates shall not be closed: 'I will go before you, and I will level the roads; I will shatter gates of bronze, and I will hew bars of iron to pieces.' "

The Greeks, although they warred against the Persians, deemed Cyrus "a worthy ruler and lawgiver." Herodotus, after visiting Persia, reported that Cyrus's reputation far outshone that of his two immediate successors: "The Persians say that Darius was a huckster, Cambyses a master, and Cyrus a father, for Darius looked to making a gain in everything. Cambyses was harsh and reckless, while Cyrus was gentle and provided them with all manner of goods."

The gentleness of Cyrus seems to have extended to his treatment of vanquished enemies. Many chroniclers assert that Cyrus displayed a radically new approach to the politics of conquest. He not only deviated from the traditional practice of slaughtering defeated kings as part of his victory celebrations but is said to have allowed Astyages, Croesus, and other deposed rulers to take up important posts within the imperial court. The Greek author-historian Bacchylides, who was born late in the sixth century BC, when the fall of the Lydian empire was still well within living memory, reported how Croesus, despairing after his unexpected defeat at Cyrus's hands, had tried to commit suicide. He leaped into a fire, but the Persian king himself snatched Croesus from the flames.

Acquiring and controlling an empire that sprawled 2,500 miles across mountains, marshland, and desert required considerable administrative efficiency. Herodotus calculated, for instance, that it took Cyrus three months to march his army from Susa in southern Iran to Sardis in Lydia, a journey of some 1,700 miles.

To ensure the efficient flow of information between the king, the provincial governors, and the powerful functionaries known as the King's Eyes and Ears who operated in distant places, Cyrus devised a sophisticated communications network. Xenophon reports that "Cyrus first ascertained how far a horse could travel in one day without being overridden, and then he had a series of posting stations built, one day's ride apart. He set up relays of horses, grooms to take care of them, and a proper man in charge of each station to receive the dispatches and hand them on, take over the jaded horses and men, and furnish fresh ones." When the message was so urgent that the relay did not halt at night, "The night messenger relieves the day messenger and rides on. Some say that when this is done, the post travels more quickly than the crane can fly."

While Cyrus was on the move, much of the court probably traveled with him. The official archives and the bureaucrats who tended them, however, remained in Susa, in conquered Babylon, or in the former Median stronghold of Ecbatana, which Cyrus took over as a summer residence.

The only intact large-scale relief at Pasargadae, this figure—wearing an Elamite robe—once guarded the gateway to Cyrus's palace. Aspects of the sculpture suggest the cultural influences at work in the king's vast empire. The crown, composed partly of curving ram's horns and upright cobras, seems to have been based on a Syrian or Phoenician model, which apparently had been derived from an Egyptian prototype. The figure's wings hark back, in turn, to Assyrian and Babylonian sculptures.

Two of the four porticoes that gave entry to Cyrus's Audience Hall at Pasargadae are seen in this reconstruction by architect Friedrich Krefter. Within the building lay a chamber 107 by 72 feet, with stone columns two stories high. Only one still stands, the nesting place of a stork.

Cyrus's throne, made of blocks of black stone, can be seen to the left of the two partial columns above in the ruins of the grand hall of his residence, Palace P, at Pasargadae. An enigmatic tower structure, the Zendan, rises behind it, and beyond looms Throne Hill.

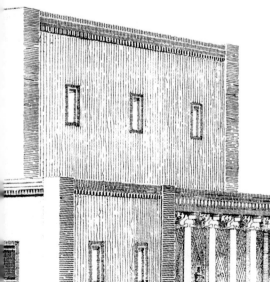

Then sometime around 547 BC, Cyrus saw fit to create a new capital of his own, at Pasargadae.

According to Strabo, Cyrus "held Pasargadae in honor because there he conquered Astyages the Mede in his last battle, transferred to himself the empire of Asia, founded a city, and constructed a palace as a memorial of his victory." Herodotus, however, suggests that the king favored Pasargadae because it was the home territory of his ancestral clan.

Pasargadae's relatively remote site in a mountain-ringed valley, 6,200 feet above sea level in the north of the province of Fars, has proved a blessing for archaeologists. While so many ancient cities have been buried almost irretrievably beneath the layers of later settlement, Cyrus's capital, despite a number of Islamic-era structures, remained reasonably accessible to the excavator.

Following Alexander the Great, other Western visitors found their way to Pasargadae and mused upon its ruins, although for a time, the association between the desolate site and Cyrus seems to have been forgotten. A 15th-century Venetian, Josafat Barbaro, wrote that the monument believed by Alexander to be Cyrus's tomb was known locally as the Tomb of Solomon's Mother. Albrecht von Mandelso, a 17th-century traveler, was told by a community of Carmelite monks in the Persian city of Shiraz that the woman was not Bathsheba, mother of King Solomon. It was instead the resting place of the parent of a caliph, or Islamic king, named Sulaiman.

In 1812 an English traveler, James Morier, published an account of his visit and supplied the first detailed description of other architectural remains on the site. Identifying a temple and

FROM THE ROYAL PERSIANS, EARTHLY VISIONS OF PARADISE

The Persians gave the world the word "paradise." To them paradise was a *paradeisos*—or enclosure—a walled park or garden. In their arid land, a well-watered green space filled with trees and shrubs was to be savored and enjoyed. Not surprisingly, Persian kings had gardens created for their pleasure. According to Xenophon, Cyrus the Younger (son of Darius II) led the Spartan general Lysander through his garden at Sardis. Laid out with geometric precision, it consisted of arrow-straight paths and beds—everything "exact and arranged in right angles"—and over all hung the "intoxicating" scent of flowers. Impressed, Lysander praised the architect, ignorant that Cyrus was responsible. The pleased prince let on that he had designed the garden and had even planted part of it.

Cyrus's love of gardens may be traced back to Cyrus the Great, who had had a new capital built at Pasargadae. There, a throne was placed in Palace P's portico *(drawing)*, so he could gaze down a large inner garden, divided into quadrants perhaps intended to reflect the empire's four quarters. But Cyrus did not live to see the project completed. Killed in battle, he came to be buried in a nearby tomb, surrounded by another garden.

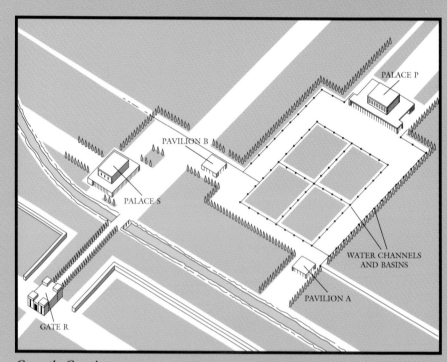

Cyrus the Great's two palaces at Pasargadae, designated by archaeologists as P and S, stood in gardens, as the ground plan above shows. Broad pathways facilitated strolling, while two airy pavilions encouraged contemplative viewing. Water running in channels beside the paths kept the main garden moist and also added a glittering, fluid element. At right is one of the basins of well-cut stone through which the water flowed.

The Persian love of plants and trees is manifest in the detail above, taken from a staircase found at Persepolis. The vegetation is highly stylized, making identification difficult.

صيد ياز وصيد يوز او شاه ذكر وسجع ع

In the centuries that followed the demise of the Persian empire, the passion for gardens continued unchecked, as the scene above from an AD 1341 illuminated manuscript and the 18th-century carpet at left illustrate. The weaver divided his garden into squares, perhaps an echo of the ground plan of Cyrus the Great's four-sectioned inner garden at Pasargadae.

a fort, he published his own copy of a cuneiform inscription found among the ruins. Morier remarked upon the striking resemblance between the tomb and descriptions by classical authors of Cyrus's sepulcher. But so convinced was he that the king's fabled capital lay much farther south, it was left to later explorers to assert that this place indeed was Pasargadae and the tomb Cyrus's, a belief held by most scholars today.

After a flood of 19th-century Europeans had come and gone, copying inscriptions, drawing plans, and making photographic records, German archaeologist Ernst Herzfeld began excavating Pasargadae in 1928. Aided only by an architect, he conducted soundings of five major monuments. After cutting exploratory trenches, he studied the evidence they afforded and soon established the ground plan for the two principal palaces and the East Gate. He exposed fragments of bas-reliefs, columns, and capitals, as well as the smashed remnants of giant statues with human and animal heads.

Other investigations followed. In 1935, German archaeologist Erich F. Schmidt led a pioneering survey of Pasargadae from the air. Fourteen years later, Ali Sami of the Iranian Archaeological Institute resumed the excavation at the site of the two palaces and cleared the area around Cyrus's tomb. When British archaeologist David Stronach launched an extensive series of digs at Pasargadae in 1961, he looked for elements of the Persian monarch's tastes, style, and attitudes toward kingship in the broken stones of his planned capital.

First he had to ascertain which monuments actually dated from the reign of Cyrus. Some clues were provided by the techniques and tools employed by the builders. The presence on stonework, for instance, of marks made by a clawed or toothed chisel—probably with a hammerlike handle—was one useful indicator, since this implement seems to have entered the Persian stonemason's tool kit only after Cyrus's death in 529 BC. Other evidence came from some of the architectural styles and ornamental motifs employed by Pasargadae's builders, which reflected the influence, and perhaps the actual hands, of Western craftsmen from Lydia or Ionia. It was likely, Stronach concluded, that buildings displaying such decorative details had been commissioned after Cyrus's conquest of the Lydians and their Greek Ionian subjects.

Such occidental influences were apparent at the Tomb of Cyrus, the most prominent monument at Pasargadae. Stronach identified Lydian and Ionian building techniques in the finely worked

masonry, fitted together with precision and held with iron clamps. The burial chamber, a small room roofed with large slabs of stone covering horizontal courses of masonry, bore a strong resemblance to the tomb of the Lydian king Alyattes in Sardis, and it was almost identical in size. The combination of these borrowings with oriental styles had resulted in a multicultural architectural entity that could now be identified as peculiarly Achaemenid.

Among the structures where the oriental influence is stronger is a monumental gate sometimes called the Palace with the Relief. Each of the two major doors was guarded by two huge, sculpted, winged bulls, derived from the magical bestiary of Assyria. Presiding over the massive building is a relief about nine feet high in the form of a supernatural being with four wings, whose features and costume combined several different Middle Eastern traditions *(page 60)*.

Grand gates like this seem to have served as a setting for the rituals of Persian kingship. A similar structure excavated in Persepolis, the capital of later Achaemenid kings, included a stone throne, suggesting that this is where the monarch held public audiences.

Certain structures at Pasargadae were harder to identify. An edifice known as the Tall-i-Takht, or Throne Hill, consists of a gigantic stone platform, constructed in a style characteristic of Lydian and east Greek masonry. It appeared to be the base for a building that was never finished, possibly a royal residence. By the early fifth cen-

From the air, the ruined walls of Tall-i-Takht, or Throne Hill, at Pasargadae seem so grandly conceived that David Stronach suggested they belonged to an unfinished palace for Cyrus, not a fortress, as some scholars had thought. Close up (right), the masonry displays a fine hand; mason marks—identifying individual work groups—are visible on the middle block; others are reproduced below in gold. The holes were gouged by scavengers seeking the iron clamps that joined the stones.

tury BC, it had been adapted to more utilitarian purposes, as indicated by the traces of work and storage space within the enclosure.

Stronach continued his predecessors' investigation of Palace S, also known as the "Palace with the Column," which may have provided a setting for court ceremonies and formal audiences. With its colonnaded porticoes, the building is reminiscent of the handsome rectangular temples of Greece and the palaces of Anatolia. At its center lay a lofty, imposing audience hall, no doubt intended to impress the parade of envoys, vassals, and tribute bearers who came to pay their respects to the sovereign.

Cyrus also ordered the building of a second palace, known to the excavators as Palace P, which even in its ruined state conveys a more intimate atmosphere. This palace too had a central hall, but the scale of the building was smaller. Its doorways were narrower; its central columns of black and white stones were shorter. Outside this hall lay a long, deep, well-shaded portico. A built-in throne was positioned to give the king, in his quiet moments, a view of what must have been Pasargadae's finest feature, its royal gardens *(page 62)*.

These gardens made a lush and fragrant setting for Cyrus's tomb; the second-century-AD Roman chronicler Arrian speaks of its "deep grass" and a "grove of all kinds of trees." The planners had tried, in their design, to reflect the order and harmony of the king's new palaces by laying down formal, rectilinear beds and broad, straight paths. To keep the plants and flowers green and sweet, water flowed through a network of some 3,600 feet of stone conduits into handsome square basins, hewed from a single block of dressed stone.

Within this paradise lay two small pavilions. In the course of excavating one of these, the archaeologists came upon a treasure that had been deliberately hidden. It was concealed within the remains of a tall water jar, made in a traditional Achaemenid design of the pottery known as buffware. More than two millennia of farmers' plows had destroyed two-thirds of the 24-inch-high vessel. Inside the surviving section of the container, however, below a thick layer of earth, lay 1,162 objects that some long-ago resident of Pasargadae prized highly enough to hide in a jar, and bury.

The hoard included many pieces of beautifully crafted jewelry, such as bracelets, earrings, pendants, necklaces, and intricately carved beads of gold, carnelian, coral, amethyst, and lapis lazuli. These were wrought in the forms of beasts, bells, flowers, geometric shapes, or the heads of gods and humans. Someone had carefully tied

A humble Achaemenid water jar (above) holds a treasure uncovered by archaeologists excavating a garden pavilion at Pasargadae. Inside, 1,162 objects had been stashed, among them a subsequently reconstructed necklace of pearls with dangling gold bell (above, right). The finely wrought gold-mesh earring (above, far right), one of a pair in the cache (visible in the jar), sports an oval piece of wire-encased lapis lazuli. In design it is similar to Etruscan earrings from the fourth century BC.

together matching pairs of earrings and other ornaments, which still lay side by side, although the filaments that once bound them had long since rotted away.

Dating the hoard posed a challenge, especially since subsequent plowing had obliterated the ground surface below which the jar was buried. The jar itself was the kind of coarse, utilitarian object that could have been made anytime between the sixth and third centuries BC. The styles of the jewelry and other valuables within it were equally hard to place. But, after a close scrutiny of such details as the beards and horns of the miniature human and animal heads, the archaeologists concluded that some of the articles may have been heirlooms of considerable age when they were hidden. The jar itself had probably been concealed sometime in the middle or late fourth century BC, perhaps by a woman of the court during the last days of the Achaemenid dynasty, fleeing in terror as Alexander's armies marched into Persia.

Cyrus did not live to finish the construction of his handsome new capital. But the cosmopolitanism of Pasargadae, based on the inspiration of architects, artisans, and sculptors from many different traditions, survives as a testament to Cyrus's sense of himself not only as a Persian king but as the lord of a truly international empire.

He was still building this domain when he died in 529 BC. Ancient writers disagree as to the moment and manner of his death. Xenophon, who had his own narrative purposes to serve, opted for a peaceable demise, with plenty of time for words of wisdom and farewell messages to followers and family, among them, supposedly,

"Remember my last saying: 'Show kindness to your friends, and then you shall have it in your power to chastise your enemies.' "

Virtually every other chronicler, however, asserted that the Persian king died in the thick of battle. Herodotus, observing the many different versions of Cyrus's end, selected one that he considered likely to be closest to the truth. In this account, Cyrus was engaged in a campaign on the northeastern frontier of his empire, on the banks of the Jaxartes River in Central Asia. On the far side of the river lay the domain of the Massagetai, a hostile tribe ruled by a warrior-queen named Tomyris. Cyrus led his army across the river, set up camp, and then proceeded to lay a trap for his opponents. He ordered the cooks and army servants to unpack huge stores of food and wine and place them conspicuously about the campsite. Then, quietly, he commanded the entire army to withdraw to some unknown location, possibly back on the Persian side of the river, where they would go undetected. A division of Tomyris's army, led by her son Spargapises, invaded the abandoned Persian camp and set upon the rations. Suddenly, the Persians reappeared and overwhelmed the raiders, who were too tipsy and full of food to stand up to their enemies. Spargapises, humiliated, promptly committed suicide.

Outraged at the trick, Tomyris sent the rest of her army against Cyrus. The engagement began as a clash between the archers, then moved into hand-to-hand combat. Most of the Persians died, including their king. Herodotus ends the tale with a grisly anecdote of Tomyris wading through the sea of corpses on the battlefield, cutting the head off Cyrus's corpse, then soaking the skull in gore, because, she declared, his hunger for blood could not be sated.

By September 529 BC, Cyrus's son Cambyses II had ascended the throne. Four years later he launched the enterprise that was to extend the vast Persian empire even farther by attacking Egypt, the most distant of the great powers of his day. This ancient and, at one time, virtually invincible kingdom had fallen into decline. A new pharaoh, Psamtik III, now reigned, but his subjects found him as unattractive as they had his father, who had preferred Greeks and other foreigners in his court over his native subjects. Corruption was endemic throughout the realm. A high-ranking officer from the Egyptian army was among Cambyses' informers, and the Persian king knew that loyalty to the Egyptian crown was shaky.

This two-foot-tall, 2,500-year-old green basalt statue—the head is a modern restoration—of Egyptian dignitary Udjahorresne bears hieroglyphic inscriptions extolling his support for Persia's King Cambyses, conqueror of Egypt. By bestowing on Cambyses the title Son of Re, Udjahorresne established a divine Egyptian lineage for the foreigner. After Udjahorresne's death, a cult devoted to him sprang up.

Early in 525 BC, Cambyses invaded from Gaza, relying on the help of local nomads, who had no love for Egypt, to get his army safely across the Sinai. At Pelusium, they met the pharaoh's army in battle and defeated it. Herodotus, who visited the battlefield 75 years after this victory, claims he saw the well-picked bones of the dead still lying where they had fallen. The triumphant Persians marched along the Nile to the capital city of Memphis, and after some ineffectual resistance by Psamtik, they took both city and king. By late spring, Cambyses arrived, triumphant, at Sais in the Nile Delta. Egyptian chroniclers, many of whom, unsurprisingly, paint the Persian conqueror as a brutal madman, report that his troops burst into the temple and profaned it.

For much of what occurred, there is the word of an eyewitness and participant in these events: Udjahorresne, who occupied a high place in the Egyptian establishment. He was Keeper of the Temple of Neith at Sais, a senior court physician, a royal chancellor, and commander of the pharaoh's navy. So eager was he to ensure that history receive his own self-justifying version of the story he had a short autobiography inscribed in hieroglyphics on his green basalt memorial statue, which now stands in the Vatican Museum in Rome.

Although Udjahorresne makes note here of "the great misfortune which had befallen the entire land" and also refers to the presence of foreign troops encamped in his temple precincts, he collaborated with the conquerors. He became an adviser to Cambyses, who had decided that the best way to retain his hold over the country was to have himself crowned Egypt's new pharaoh. Udjahorresne counseled him in the process and drew up the set of formal titles that established Cambyses on the throne. To confer legitimacy upon his claim, Cambyses let it be known that he, in the manner of all Egypt's kings, was also the son of one of its deities. Presumably on the advice of Udjahorresne, he revealed himself as Mesuti-Re, offspring of the sun god.

Udjahorresne does not hide the fact that the new pharaoh and demigod showed his appreciation by promoting and honoring the Keeper of the Temple. He also tells us that Cambyses took pains to repair the shrine and make good any damage inflicted by his soldiers during the occupation. In the course of organizing his Egyptian administration, however, Cambyses enraged the priestly hierarchy by interfering with the finances of Egypt's temples, which had traditionally enjoyed massive economic power. To help defray the cost of conquest, he issued a decree, preserved in a third-century-BC papyrus copy, reducing and diverting temple revenues, and imposing various economies upon the privileged religious elite.

After three years spent establishing Persian control of Egypt, Cambyses left his new dominion. On the journey home, or soon thereafter, he died. The circumstances are mysterious, and as in his father's case, there are several versions of Cambyses' death. One chronicler, the fifth-century-BC Greek physician Ctesias, relates that Cambyses, back in Babylon, was whittling a piece of wood with his short sword to pass the time when he stabbed himself in the thigh. He died 11 days later. Other texts, however, say that the death occurred while traveling through Syria, at a place called Ecbatana, the same name as the Median capital, an all-too-neat twist of fate, since it was allegedly foretold that he would die in Ecbatana.

Many scholars believe that it was Cyrus's distant relative and Cambyses' successor, Darius I, who added to the structures at Pasargadae the inscriptions in the name of "Cyrus, an Achaemenid." They suspect that this was a fiction invented by Darius, who claimed to be of royal Achaemenid blood but was not the direct descendant of the empire's founder, Cyrus II. In this way, Darius was able to establish a link with Cyrus through their supposed common ancestor, Achaemenes, possibly a seventh-century-BC king of Persia.

The aftermath of Cambyses' death was set in stone by Darius. On a cliff face at Behistun in the Zagros Mountains, 340 feet above the ancient road from Mesopotamia to Ecbatana, his sculptors and scribes created a relief that, in word and picture,

documented the complex web of rebellion and conspiracy that had brought Darius to the throne. Darius ordered the text to be inscribed in the three most important languages of his realm: Old Persian;

"Now do you believe what I have done?" Darius I's words seemed almost to taunt American historian and linguist George C. Cameron as he risked life and limb in 1948 to study firsthand the king's inscriptions chiseled into a cliff 340 feet above Iran's rocky Behistun plain. Cameron's goal was to copy and photograph them; transcribe four columns of hitherto inaccessible text; make latex molds, like those seen partially covering the 10-

Suspended from steel cables and guided by ropes, the scaffold is lowered into position in front of the panels. Water seeping from the limestone mountain had eroded some of the inscriptions, but preserved others by coating them with sediment. By removing the crust with gentle taps of his hammer, Cameron revealed new writings.

by-18-foot central panel at left; and figure out how the sculptors had reached the wall 2,500 years ago. There, the Persians completed one of the greatest self-advertisements of all time, which proclaimed in three tongues Darius's triumph over his 10 enemies.

An oil company operating close by helped by drilling holes into the cliff 200 feet above the panels and inserting steel pins. These allowed Cameron to suspend cables for a scaffold. Still, to get to the platform, he and his two assistants had to climb down part of the rock face and then descend a 30-foot ladder. Outcrops made raising and lowering the scaffold difficult. In his explorations, Cameron dis-

covered that the ancient sculptors had reached their perches by steps they chiseled away when the work was finished.

As the days wore on, Cameron and his men were assaulted by cold and rain. To keep warm, he wore two pairs of pants, a wool shirt and sweater, an army coat, a sheepskin jacket, and a blanket. Creating the mold involved applying five layers of latex, to which burlap and gauze were added for body. Sometimes Cameron had to lean from the ends of the scaffold, which had no guardrails. Once, he nearly fell, pulled back in the nick of time by his 14-year-old son Tom. "Dad," teased the boy, "if you fall, I'll never speak to you again!"

Cameron's son Tom measures one of the narrow ledges on which the carvers stood. His father was working on just such a ledge when a loosened boulder came crashing down, showering the scholar—who had thrown himself against the wall—with fragments.

Akkadian, the language of Babylon; and Elamite. An Aramaic copy, written on papyrus, was also found at Elephantine in Egypt.

This desire on the part of Darius to write an immutable history of his ascent to power led, some 2,400 years later, to a major breakthrough in the study of the ancient world. For the trilingual text at Behistun would play as significant a part in the translation of cuneiform as the Rosetta stone had played in the decipherment of Egyptian hieroglyphics.

The man who did most to crack the code was Henry Rawlinson, a British scholar and soldier. Rawlinson paid many visits to Behistun between 1835 and 1847. Climbing up the stony face, dangling from ropes, inching along ledges, and balancing precariously on boards and ladders, Rawlinson and a young helper—to whom he refers, in his memoirs, only as "a wild Kurdish boy"—managed to copy most of the inscriptions.

To decipher the Old Persian text, Rawlinson combined brilliant guesswork, the knowledge of the names and genealogy of the Achaemenid royal house supplied by Herodotus, and a painstaking study of the *Zend Avesta*. The latter is a compilation of the sacred scriptures of Zoroastrianism, the ancient Persian religion. One of the oldest surviving versions of the *Zend Avesta* known to Rawlinson was written in an early form of Persian. By a slow and careful sequence of comparisons, Rawlinson used it and the names of the kings as a pathway into the Old Persian text. In 1849, after another two years of work, he succeeded in deciphering much of the Babylonian translation of Darius's narrative.

In an attempt to verify the claims of Rawlinson and others who had been working on decoding cuneiform, a committee was set up to test the methods that seemed to be working: Four scholars, including Rawlinson, were invited to decipher another cuneiform text. When the four translations were compared in 1857, they proved to be very similar, and the committee concluded that the techniques used were correct.

The previously locked gates of undeciphered cuneiform now flew open to reveal the chronicles of the ancient Middle East, a treasure of myths, laws, religious rituals, documents of public administration, and details about personalities and everyday life—a store of knowledge that would change forever humanity's collective image of its early years on earth.

PERSEPOLIS: A GHOSTLY GRANDEUR

So vast were the riches assembled and displayed at Persepolis it was written that its conqueror, Alexander the Great, required "10,000 pairs of mules and 5,000 camels" to carry everything away. What could not be removed, the Greek biographer Plutarch relates, was put to the torch. Columns, capitals, joists, and beams exquisitely fashioned from Lebanese cedar went up in flames, along with any furniture, tapestries, and other combustibles that Alexander's plundering troops may have left behind. Wood roofs crashed to the ground in showers of ash and ember, and soon only those columns, doorways, reliefs, and sculptures that had been hewed from stone remained standing, and many of these toppled later in earthquakes. Experts suspect that most of the mudbrick walls also survived the conflagration, but centuries of scouring summer sandstorms were to reduce them gradually to dust.

Accumulating at the site, windblown dust and sand covered ashes and ruins alike, burying them beneath a layer as much as 26 feet deep and sparing them from the ravages of time and marauder. The ashes, finally uncovered after 1931 by excavators from the Oriental Institute of the University of Chicago under the direction of the pioneering archaeologist Ernst Herzfeld and later that of Erich F. Schmidt, would corroborate Plutarch's account of the blaze. And much of the sculpture would be so well preserved that the institute's executive secretary could describe it in 1933 "as clean, sharp, and fresh-looking as though chiseled yesterday."

However battered they may be around the edges, the pair of stairway reliefs pictured above are good examples. Together with carvings discovered on the doorjambs of Darius I's Palace, visible at upper left, and especially on the remarkable monumental stairways of his Apadana, or audience hall, whose columns are at upper right, they would almost double the world's existing collection of ancient Persian art.

A PAST AWAITING DISCOVERY

When Ernst Herzfeld climbed the Mountain of Mercy to take the snapshots joined together below, he could hardly have dreamed of the riches that awaited Persepolis's excavators. Thick walls pointed to fortifications; doorways and windows delineated once-opulent chambers; and columns evoked halls with lofty ceilings. Years of backbreaking digging, however, would be required to bare such finds as 20,000 cuneiform tablets or the grand stairways of the Apadana and Council Hall. Where the staircase friezes poked above ground, they had been damaged; below ground they were in almost pristine shape.

The sculpted head above belonged to one of a pair of immense stone bulls that guarded the portico at the north end of the Hall of 100 Columns.

PALACE OF XERXES I   PALACE OF DARIUS I   APADANA

COUNCIL HALL   HALL OF 100 COLUMNS

GATE OF XERXES

Above, identical images of a king—probably Artaxerxes I—top two door-jambs at the south end of the rubble-strewn Hall of 100 Columns.

UNFINISHED GATE

NORTHERN FORTIFICATIONS

REMOVING THE DUST OF TIME

Hundreds of villagers were recruited to do the spadework and sifting that the project required, and a few were trained to act as foremen. Summoned at sunrise by a makeshift gong—a steel plate suspended from a wood post and struck with a mallet— the workers began each day with a song and labored until sunset, taking off half an hour for a lunch of bread, cheese, water, and goat's milk or yogurt.

Above, dust rises from the Mountain of Mercy as diggers expose the eastern fortifications. Carts were used to haul earth to a dumpsite.

Below, workers uncover chambers lying between the Hall of 100 Columns on the right and the already cleared north hall of the Treasury.

Earthquakes scattered many of the Apadana's reliefs and other carved stone pieces. Using rope, wooden planks, and muscle power, workers dragged the heavy chunks up the northern stairway (above). Below, a large tripod is employed to set fallen reliefs from the eastern stairway in place.

SETTING UP SHOP IN A HAREM

After sleeping in tents for two seasons, Herzfeld and his team finally found comfortable accommodations in 1933 in the edifice shown here, known then as the Harem of Xerxes I, which the architect Friedrich Krefter turned into the expedition's workrooms and living quarters. Herzfeld's two dogs had the run of the place, as did Krefter's Airedale. And at night, after the sounds of the workday had died away, Herzfeld, Krefter, another architect, and a draftsman gathered in a rug-draped chamber, took up violins, a viola, and a cello, and let the music of a string quartet mingle with the clanking bells of passing camel caravans.

Above, carved stone windows and doorways with fluted lintels ring eight column bases in the north portico of the Harem. Oriental Institute builders re-created the deteriorated walls and placed new columns and capitals atop the bases as part of the restoration of the building (below).

Workers sort sherds in the rebuilt Harem. Since pieces of stone columns were not found in this area of the site, architects concluded that the originals had to have been made of wood.

BUILDINGS THAT ROSE FROM THE ASHES

Almost 30 years after Friedrich Krefter departed from Persepolis in 1935, the ancient capital again seized the architect's imagination. Drawing on his experiences with Herzfeld, and on the results both of Herzfeld's successor Erich Schmidt and of subsequent Iranian and Italian excavators, Krefter penned a series of detailed and sweeping reconstructions that transformed such desolate tableaux as the one at right into scenes of kingly grandeur. Three of the renderings are reprinted here.

Photographed from the north at the start of excavations, some of the Apadana's 13 surviving columns dwarf the archaeologists' tents.

In Friedrich Krefter's reconstruction below, troops muster on the plain to the west of Persepolis. The double stairway at the head of the formation leads to the Gate of Xerxes, through which all visitors were obliged to pass to reach the Apadana, the large square building at the center of the illustration.

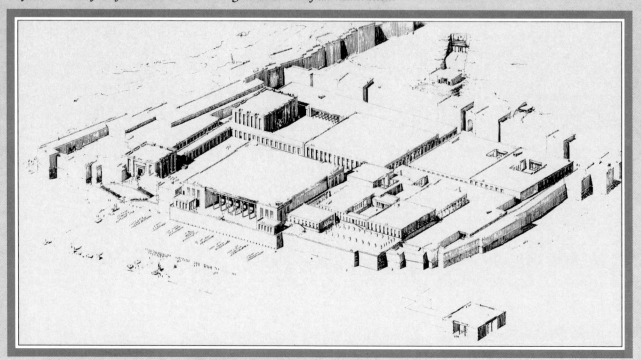

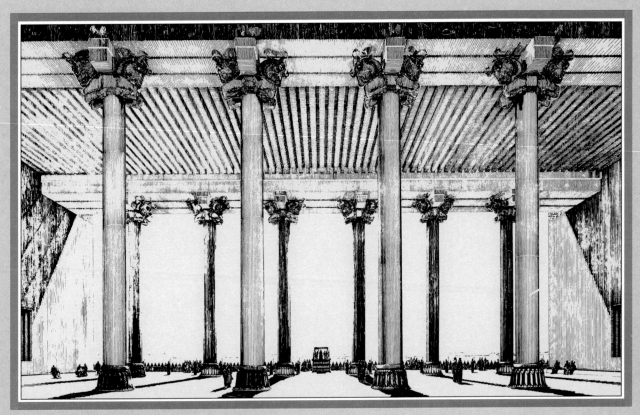

Topped with bulls' heads, 60-foot-tall columns brace the beamed ceiling of the Apadana's west portico, depicted by Krefter from within its central hall.

Krefter's drawing (below) features monumental carved stairways leading to the Apadana's east portico and the main entrance of the Council Hall.

Its full extent revealed by decades of digging and restoration, Persepolis still projects might and grandeur in this photograph made in the 1970s. An Italian team labored to conserve and stabilize many of the surviving structures on the rectangular foundation that underlay the city.

THE DAZZLING REACH OF DARIUS'S IMPERIAL SPEAR

Enthroned in Persepolis, the magnificent city he built, Darius I firmly grasps the royal scepter in his right hand. In his left he holds a lotus blossom with two buds, symbolic of royalty.

During the construction of the Suez Canal, workers digging 20 miles north of Suez in 1866 came upon fragments of a red granite stele that, whole, had stood nearly 10 feet tall and measured about seven feet across. Startled at finding the monument, the men would have been even more surprised had they been able to read the inscriptions on its sides, spelled out in Old Persian, Babylonian, Elamite, and Egyptian. These included an astonishing message—repeated in all four tongues—from Darius the Great, King of Persia: "I ordered this canal to be dug from the Nile, which flows in Egypt, to the sea that goes to Persia."

Scholars had read the Greek historian Herodotus's account of the great canal built by Darius I, but they had dismissed it as romanticized fiction. Now the pickax supported the assertions of his pen—or stylus. According to the Greek, Darius learned that an Egyptian pharaoh had tried to dig a canal from the Nile to the Gulf of Suez a century earlier, only to give up because of the high cost of the project in human lives. Aware of the strategic and economic importance of improving the sea links around his empire's shores, Darius brought the task to a successful conclusion. "This canal was dug out as I commanded," he boasts on his stele, "and ships went from Egypt through this canal into Persia as was my desire."

The hieroglyphic text describes the ceremonies at the waterway's official opening. Many important functionaries had been invited, and perhaps 32 ships sailed through the canal bearing tribute. Their safe arrival in Persia was duly reported. Speeches extolling Darius's achievements were noted in the text, which concluded with the acknowledgment that "never was the like done before."

Stretching 125 miles, the channel included about 35 miles of natural waterway through the Bitter Lakes of the Sinai Peninsula. According to Herodotus, the canal itself was wide enough for two war galleys to pass each other under oar, an estimated 80 feet. Ships took four days to move from one end to the other.

Additional evidence of the canal's existence is provided by three other inscribed steles that had once lined the waterway. Two of these were also discovered by workmen during the construction of the modern canal in the 1860s. A third was found at a location discovered earlier by Napoleon Bonaparte's troops in 1799; an 1884 excavation of the site by French archaeologist Clermont Ganneau turned up 25 fragments of the stele, and these were turned over to the Louvre, where subsequently they mysteriously disappeared.

At least one modern scholar has characterized the ancient canal as the greatest achievement of Darius's 36-year reign, but in fact his was an age so full of accomplishments it is hard to set any one above the other. The empire that Darius acquired and extended united western Asia from the Mediterranean to the Indus Valley under a single monarch. Its territories stretched from the foothills of the Himalayas all the way to the Aegean Sea and the sands of the North African desert. Covering an area of almost two million square miles, it had some 10 million inhabitants.

As ruler of an empire greater than any the world had yet known Darius could afford to brag, as he did on his tomb. Beneath his own image, which showed him standing on a dais borne by representative figures of 30 of his subject peoples, ran the legend: "If now thou shalt think, 'How many are the countries which King Darius held?' look at the sculptures [of those] who bear the throne. Then shalt thou know, then shall it become known to thee: The spear of a Persian man has gone far."

Even Darius's Greek enemies were willing to call him the Great, an accolade that did not rest simply on his military abilities. While his predecessors—Cyrus II and his son Cambyses II—had been occupied with conquering, Darius devoted much of his energy to building the structures of imperial government. He continued the

In this photograph taken in 1939, Iranian crews directed by members of the University of Chicago's Oriental Institute excavate a limestone tower constructed by Darius I at Naqsh-i Rustam, four miles north of Persepolis. Although scholars are still unsure of its purpose, the tower may have been erected as a tomb or used in religious rituals. The building, more than 40 feet tall, contains one room approached by a stairway.

tradition, established by Cyrus, of ruling to an impressive degree with the cooperation of local rulers. Those who accepted Persian overlordship were often left in place, and the religions and customs of subject peoples were respected. The clay tablets of Darius's scribes could well be organized into a textbook of judicious administration.

The economies of regions throughout the Middle East flourished in the peace imposed by Persian arms. Revenue flowed into the royal treasuries, but much of this tribute paid for great works, among them the splendid royal city of Persepolis deep in the Achaemenid heartland.

Darius also had the venerable Elamite capital city of Susa renovated and improved. In 1929, French archaeologists had direct evidence of this at a palace he had had erected. There they found inscribed clay tablets commemorating the construction of the building

and its grand, 36-columned apadana, or audience hall. Known today as the Foundation Charter of
Susa, these itemize the riches that
had gone into Darius's magnificent structure. Cedarwood had
been brought from Lebanon, the
text asserted, and other timber
from Carmania, or Kerman, in
southern Persia, and from Gan-
dhara in today's Afghanistan.
Gold came both from Sardis in
Lydia and from Bactria, 1,000
miles away beside the Oxus River
in the foothills of the Hindu Kush in Uzbekistan. Ivory was imported not just from the king's African domains of Egypt and Ethiopia
but also from Sind on the threshold of India.

*In a watercolor painted in 1913 by
French architect and archaeologist Maurice Pillet, Darius I leads a procession
of servants and guards into a chamber of
his stone-columned palace at Susa.
Born in 1881, Pillet traveled in the Middle East and worked for the French expedition at Susa. He included the glazed-
brick frieze of archers after seeing it reconstructed* (right) *in Paris.*

The artisans employed in the building were also listed. There
were stonecutters from Ionia, goldsmiths from Media, brickmasons
from Babylon, and woodworkers from Egypt. The talents and resources of the whole known world, it must have seemed, had been
pooled to produce a monument worthy of the great king.

The system of government Darius created would eventually
stiffen into rigidity, leaving the realm exposed to the assault of a new,
still-more-ambitious conqueror from the West, Alexander the Great.
Given the primitive communications of the time, the extraordinary
thing is not that so vast an empire eventually fell, but that it survived,
largely intact, for 150 years after his death.

Glimpses of Darius the man come from his monuments and
from the hearsay descriptions of Greek historians. It seems, for example, that he was of medium build. His image on the cliff face at
Behistun *(pages 70-71),* usually described as life-size, stands 5 feet 8
inches tall; although this in itself can hardly be considered hard evidence, the dimensions of his tomb at Naqsh-i Rustam *(pages 102-
103)* near Persepolis provide some confirmation, indicating that he
probably was not more than 5 foot 10. According to a later Greek
commentator, the physician Polykritos, who served at the Persian
court in the early fourth century BC, Darius was a strikingly handsome man, possessed of a trait that was considered a mark of distinction at the time—long arms reaching down to his knees.

In temperament Darius was dynamic, at times despotic. He could be generous to those who served him well. Herodotus tells the story of a Greek doctor, reduced to slavery by the fortunes of war, who set Darius's ankle after it had been dislocated and was rewarded with cupfuls of gold coins. Enemies, on the other hand, were often treated mercilessly; one Median pretender to the throne had his nose and ears cut off and his tongue torn out before being impaled.

While the reign of Darius I was generally a period of peace, growth, and accomplishment, there were disturbing incidents. His first task was to put down the wave of revolt that swept across the empire in the wake of the disputed succession. According to the Behistun inscription, he fought 19 battles and dispatched eight would-be kings in the course of a single year. After restoring order, however, he adopted a conciliatory policy toward the rebellious lands to win their loyalty, granting them three years' remission of taxes and a moratorium for the same period on military service obligations.

Next Darius turned his attention eastward, bringing the province of Hindush in the lower Indus Valley, in what is now Paki-

Discovered by the French expedition in the 1880s, the colorful but fragile bricks making up the frieze below were found scattered near the entrance to the palace. Jane Dieulafoy wrote of her concern regarding their excavation and shipment to the Louvre, "What terrible worries I have about the discovery and removal of the enamels . . . when moved, they break and crumble." The 3-by-13-inch bricks, made of sand and lime, then enameled in brilliant hues, were strengthened during reconstruction. Some scholars have identified the archers as members of the 10,000 Immortals, the elite Persian guard.

stan, into the empire. The acquisition was an important one, for the gold of this distant region was to make it by far the richest source of revenue in all his realm. Then in 513 BC, nine years into his reign, he sent an army over the Bosporus into Europe to launch a punitive raid against the Scythian tribes of the Black Sea's western and northern shores. By constantly moving, the tribesmen evaded his troops, who were eventually forced to return home with their mission unaccomplished. But Darius took advantage of the opportunity to subdue the provinces of Macedonia and Thrace.

There Darius established a bridgehead in Europe of later significance. Europeans—in particular the tough, independently minded Greeks who inhabited the Continent's easternmost shores—would prove an enduring thorn in the empire's side. Even so, the Greeks were not nearly as troubling to the Persians as the Persians would be to them; the presence, power, and demands of the interlopers from the east impacted heavily on them.

By the reign of Darius, there were already many Greeks within the empire, especially in the province of Ionia on the western fringe of Asia Minor. Trouble broke out in 499 BC, when the Ionians rose in revolt. The Athenians sent troops to help their rebellious cousins, and in their presence, the city of Sardis, the seat of Persian administration in the area, was burned. When the news reached Darius, his anger knew no bounds. According to Herodotus, he loosed an arrow at the sky, beseeching Ahura Mazda, chief god of the Persians, to grant him vengeance. He then gave instructions to a servant to repeat to him three times each day, "Master, remember the Athenians," lest he forget to punish their presumption.

There was not much risk of Darius's failing to do so. No sooner had the Ionian revolt been put down than he started planning an

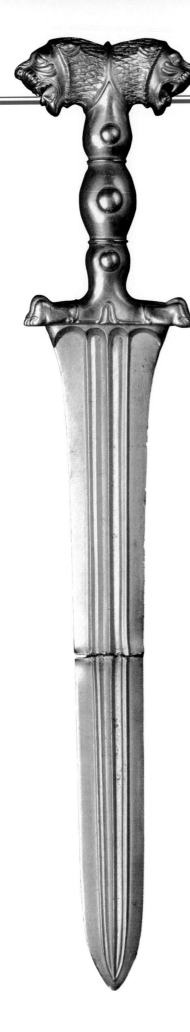

expedition to settle his score with the upstart alliance of Greek states. In 490 BC his troops landed on the mainland of Greece at Marathon, just 26 miles from Athens itself. There they found an Athenian army drawn up to meet them. Forced to fight in a cramped and exposed position, the Persians were decimated. When the navy raced to the rescue, ready to assault the city, it was only to find that the victorious Greek troops, not content to rest on their laurels, had immediately marched back and were waiting there to resist a landing. Frustrated, the Persian commanders had no option but to return home across the Aegean. While the Greeks celebrated a great victory, Darius's wrath remained unappeased.

From the Persian point of view, however, the setback in Greece must have seemed slight compared with the great achievements of Darius's reign, and none of these, perhaps, was more far reaching than the king's success in institutionalizing imperial power. Cyrus II and Cambyses II had ruled by charisma and the momentum of conquest; it was Darius who set the structure they had created on a sound administrative footing.

At the apex of the pyramid of imperial command was the monarch, ruler by divine right, and the ultimate arbiter of the fate of nations. There was no single administrative center of the Achaemenid empire, for the focus of decision making was always where the king happened to be; in the words of one commentator, he "carried his capital with him."

Even the competent Darius, however, needed help to rule such a vast domain, so he divided the empire into 20 component parts, known as satrapies. The reigning governors, or satraps, were drawn from the highest ranks of the Persian nobility. Many came from the so-called Seven Families, which included Darius's own clan as well as the kin of the six men who had helped Darius establish himself on the throne. They had thereby established a hereditary right to a place in the highest echelons of the Achaemenid court.

The choice of satraps ensured that Persians maintained ultimate control of the provinces. Beneath them, however, the subdivisions of the empire, including individual regions and cities, were often ruled by local people. Non-Persians could also find favor in the higher reaches of the imperial court. Such was the destiny of the prophet Daniel, whom the Persian king—probably Cyrus—according to the biblical account, "planned to set over the whole kingdom." Another figure of the Old Testament, Nehemiah, was appointed cupbearer to a later Achaemenid monarch, Artaxerxes I, an important position in the ruler's personal circle. He was also made governor of Judea.

The satraps lived royally. As the monarch's representatives in their provinces, they were responsible for all government functions, from security and justice to economic development and the raising of taxes. The perquisites of the job were commensurate with the responsibilities. One Babylonian governor was said to have a daily income of five bushels of silver and to keep a stable of 17,000 horses.

Given their wide authority, there was always a danger that the satraps would establish their own power bases. In the later years of the empire, when the office became hereditary in some regions, revolts did occur and royal control could only be reestablished with bloodshed.

Darius himself, however, took considerable care to keep his satraps in line. He appointed secretaries directly answerable to himself to oversee their activities, and he dispatched itinerant officials, dubbed the King's Eyes and Ears, to determine whether they were administering their territories conscientiously. In addition, the army, on whose shoulders all power ultimately rested, followed a line of command that led directly to the monarch. While satraps might take control of local forces when war threatened, in peacetime the garrisons generally came under independent commanders whose allegiance was directly to the king.

To help them cope with the day-to-day business of administration, both king and satraps relied on the services of a corps of scribes whose job it was to keep the imperial records. They would have been essential even if Darius and his successors had not been illiterate, as is believed; book learning was not regarded as an aristocratic virtue. The nobility was educated, according to a traditional formula, "to ride a horse, to draw a bow, and to speak the truth." So when the monarch wished to consult the annals, he needed help. On the cliff face at Behistun, for example, Darius proclaims that the text "was inscribed and was read before me"; in the biblical book Esther, we hear that King Xerxes I, Darius's immediate successor, called for

A massive doorway crowned with the concave cornice typical of those in the Palace of Darius I at Persepolis still stands at the site of the Persian temple of Hibis in the Egyptian oasis of el-Kharga. Cambyses II, who ruled Egypt before Darius, caused widespread resentment when he attempted to diminish the importance of the country's millennia-old religion. Darius took a more conciliatory approach, building temples such as this one, whose reliefs cast Darius in the role of pharaoh.

records to be read aloud to him one night when he could not sleep.

A story in the book of Ezra from the Old Testament vouches for the efficacy of royal records. In Darius's reign the Jews in Jerusalem rebuilt the Temple, destroyed by the Babylonians 63 years earlier, without seeking prior permission from the local governor. Called to account for their action, they cited an authorization issued by Cyrus the Great. The satrap then wrote to Darius to ask whether such a decree in fact existed. A copy was duly tracked down in the repository at Ecbatana. As a result, Darius wrote back to say that the governor not only should refrain from impeding the work but should pay for it out of public funds.

The monarchs, literate or not, were well aware of the power of the written word. Darius was concerned by the lack of a script to represent the Achaemenids' own language, which scholars today call Old Persian. Since it included sounds that could not be adequately recorded in an alien form of cuneiform, he had a more appropriate script devised: The inscription at Behistun proudly proclaims, "According to the will of Ahura Mazda, I have made the writing of a different sort, in Aryan [Old Persian] which did not exist before."

Darius also took pride in meting out justice and fair dealing for all, a policy he regarded as an essential part of the business of government. His tomb inscription asserts: "Says Darius the King: By the favor of Ahura Mazda, I am of such a sort that I am a friend to right, I am not a friend to wrong; it is not my desire that the weak man should have wrong done to him by the mighty; nor is it my desire that the mighty should have wrong done to him by the weak."

Contemporary sources referred to him as Lawgiver, although no legal code bearing his name has come to light. What is

Made of gray-blue limestone and most likely sculpted in Egypt around 510 BC, this headless statue of Darius I was discovered in Susa in 1972. Its robe and pedestal bear inscriptions in Egyptian, Old Persian, Elamite, and Babylonian, all naming the king. Probably brought to Susa by Darius's son Xerxes I during a period of Egyptian rebellion, the statue was placed near the gateway leading into Darius's palace.

certain, however, is that Achaemenid rulers in general expected laws to be enforced rigidly and impartially, whether they were their own Persian laws or local statutes, which for the most part were allowed to remain in place. The biblical book Daniel speaks eloquently of "the law of the Medes and Persians which cannot be revoked," even if the monarch himself might so wish. The prophet Daniel was forced into a den of lions for an infringement of one of its statutes despite the fact that he was a favored servant of the king.

The Persian rulers could be merciless to those of their officials who failed to live up to the standard of behavior expected of them. Herodotus tells the story of a Persian judge found guilty, during Cambyses's reign, of taking a bribe to fix a case. The king had the man flayed, and he ordered that the skin be used to upholster the seat of justice in the judge's own courtroom. His son was then appointed in his place, and he was told to remember what his chair was made of when he gave his judgments.

To pay for the running of the empire, the Achaemenids relied on a carefully administered system of taxation that filled their treasuries to overflowing. Soon after his accession, Darius ordered a census of the lands in his territories, with their expected annual agricultural yield. These figures were then used to determine the revenue to be paid by each region. In Darius's day, the take was about 20 percent of the crop's value. Native Persians were granted tax-exempt status.

In addition to the monies raised in currency or precious metals, contributions in kind were requisitioned from particular provinces. Arabia annually supplied three tons of the aromatic resin frankincense, while Egypt was called upon to furnish large numbers of sheep, horses, and mules, and also a cash levy. The cruelest tribute was exacted from Babylon,

Median dignitaries carry tribute to the king as they ascend the northern stairway of the Council Hall at Persepolis. The sculptor conveys a sense of stately movement as the figures climb in lockstep. Some of the officials, in a gesture of respect, hold one hand in front of the mouth.

which had to send 500 castrated boys each year to perform as servants in the Persian aristocratic households.

Then as now, taxes were unpopular, but the financial burden may have been a relatively light price to pay for the economic benefits of the peace and prosperity under Persian rule. Trade blossomed with the improvement of communications and the removal of internal barriers, and much of the empire experienced a level of affluence it rarely, if ever, had known before.

Commerce was encouraged by the introduction of a standard coinage, a concept that had arisen in gold-rich Lydia some decades earlier. Borrowing the idea, Darius spread it throughout the western part of the empire, where networks of traders were quick to see the advantages of the innovation. The basic currency was the daric, three-quarters of an inch in diameter and consisting of one-third of an ounce of 98 percent pure gold.

The coins, which on one face bore the image of the king holding a bow, were referred to colloquially as "archers." One Greek ruler, Agesilaus II of Sparta, was called back from an expedition to Phrygia in 394 BC to face a hostile group of his neighbors; they had been bribed by the Persians to force him to abandon his military efforts against the imperial army. He joked ruefully that it had taken 10,000 archers to drive him out of Asia.

Besides encouraging the use of currency, Darius stimulated prosperity by supporting agricultural innovation. "In that you are cultivating my land, introducing food crops from across the Euphrates," he wrote to a satrap in Ionia, "I commend your policy, and for this great credit will be given you in the house of the king." Darius also took a special interest in irrigation. The ancient network of canals—fed by the Tigris and Euphrates—that served the plain between these two rivers was also expanded.

A servant in the Palace of Darius I at Persepolis stands ready, with towel and perfume bottle, to minister to the needs of his sovereign. The vast wealth accumulated by the Achaemenid kings afforded a lifestyle of extraordinary luxury that was supported by thousands of slaves.

The result was exceptionally high productivity. Herodotus, who had traveled in the region, told incredulous readers used to the poor soils of mountainous Greece: "The blades of wheat and barley are at least three inches wide. As for millet and sesame, I will not say to what astonishing size they grow, though I know well enough; but I also know that people who have not been to Babylonia have refused to believe even what I have said already about its fertility."

While all the land in the empire theoretically belonged to the king, most was in practice held by wealthy proprietors in his name. In Darius's day a feudal arrangement prevailed, by which the landed nobility provided the king with troops in time of need. But as time passed, the estates were subdivided and gradually lost their military obligations, until by the later years of the empire, the kings were dependent on foreign mercenaries for much of their fighting forces.

The feudal levies, and later the mercenary bands, supplemented a core of professional soldiers who were the main prop of Achaemenid rule. At their heart were the 10,000 Immortals, so called by the Greeks because their numbers were kept constant: Whenever a soldier was killed or disabled, another immediately took his place. All were Persian infantrymen, and from their ranks a detachment of 1,000 served as the elite royal bodyguard.

For the empire to benefit effectively from its military prowess and economic growth, good communications were essential, and in this field Darius's policies were particularly farsighted. The network of arteries connecting the main regions of the empire was extended and improved. From the Achaemenid heartland in south Persia, roads branched east across the Iranian Plateau to Bactria and India and west through Palestine to Egypt. When Cyrus's son Cambyses took the western route to invade Egypt, he had water jugs buried at intervals along the artery for the benefit of his thirsty troops.

No highway in the empire could compare, however, with the so-called Royal Road, stretching some 1,600 miles from Susa to Sardis in Asia Minor. Herodotus, who traveled part of it, reported that along its length there were at least six ferry crossings, a number of heavily guarded checkpoints, and 111 way stations providing food and shelter for journeyers, as well as for their horses and pack animals. Private travelers no doubt paid for their own lodgings, but those on official business were given their keep. Among the documents that have come down to us from Darius's time are vouchers authorizing specific individuals to claim free rations at these inns.

Security on the Royal Road was bolstered by checkpoints, staffed by military detachments, through which all travelers had to pass. Besides deterring bandits, these enabled the authorities to keep a watchful eye on traffic on the empire's principal highway. So effective was surveillance that when one exiled Greek in Susa sought to send a treasonable message urging revolt back home to the Ionian cities, he found that the only way of getting it through was to tattoo it onto a trusted slave's shaved scalp. He then waited until the man's hair had grown again before dispatching him to Sardis with instructions for his contact there to arrange a haircut on the slave's arrival.

While Darius's interests were as far-ranging as his roads, extending to every corner of his kingdom, his loyalty was to the heartland in southern Persia. It was there that he determined to leave his greatest monument, the city that Darius and his people called Persia, which was also the name of their country. Known today as Persepolis *(overleaf)*, it is located about 45 miles southwest of Pasargadae, which was built earlier by Cyrus. The ruins of Persepolis rise on the edge of a high plain ringed by barren hills. Work on it began around 509 BC and continued through the reigns of Darius's two successors. There was then a hiatus in building efforts for some 100 years, but construction resumed in the mid-fourth century BC. Throughout this period, Persepolis was the heart of the world's most powerful empire and a repository for much of its wealth. In 330 BC the city's great palace was burned to the ground by Alexander the Great, who eventually conquered the Persians, and it was never occupied again.

What remained was an imposing ruin set on a natural rock platform rising 50 feet above the level of the surrounding plain and backing onto a bare mountainside. Visible from a

The magnificence of Persian court life is illustrated by the exquisitely crafted gold rhyton below. So huge were the Persians' stores of gold that the precious metal was even carried to the battlefield, where the court assembled and continued to live royally. According to Herodotus, the booty collected by the Greek general Pausanias after the defeat of Xerxes' army included "gold and silver furniture, couches overlaid with the same precious metals; bowls, goblets, and cups, all of gold."

distance, the 13 columns, 60 feet high, that still stand once helped support the roof of the Apadana, or audience hall, an edifice of almost 40,000 square feet, reserved for ceremonial use. A monumental stone stairway, decorated with relief sculptures, continued to jut from the rubble-covered terrace through later ages, testimony to the city's former grandeur.

A stately ruin in a barren location, Persepolis bore silent witness not only to Achaemenid splendor but also to the ultimate vanity of vaunting human ambition. As such, it attracted the interest of reflective visitors from the earliest times, demonstrated by the graffiti carved on the walls of the abandoned palaces by Sassanian travelers in the fourth century AD. After the Arab conquest of Persia in AD 642, the site continued to attract visitors; Islamic geographers included detailed descriptions of the ruins in their works.

Western interest in Persepolis was aroused during the Renaissance with Europe's reawakened knowledge of the classics, in particular works about Alexander the Great, the destroyer of Darius's city. The first European accounts of the site date to the 15th century AD, although it was not until 1618 that it was definitely identified as the former Achaemenid capital.

An early attempt to excavate the ruins was made in 1878 by the governor of the province of Fars, in which the city lies. An unsavory figure, reputed to have had the hands of 700 of his subjects cut off in punishment for various offenses, the governor seems to have been motivated more by the desire to find treasure than to add to the

Morning light casts long shadows across Persepolis. In the background can be seen the tent city erected by Shah Reza Pahlavi to house dignitaries invited to the 1971 celebration of the 2,500th anniversary of the founding of the Persian empire.

store of human knowledge. Although he set some 600 laborers to work, he kept no record of what he found. One of his assistants, however, took a wider interest in the project, producing in 1896 under the pen name of Forsat a book entitled *The Relics of Persia,* which included a plan and drawings of the structures.

In 1924 a German archaeologist, Ernst Herzfeld, was invited by the Persian government to present a detailed proposal for the exploration of Persepolis. His recommendations were accepted, and in 1931, digging once again went forward at the site, this time on a scientific basis, under the auspices of the Oriental Institute of the University of Chicago. The continuing excavation, first under Herzfeld's direction and then under that of his compatriot Erich F. Schmidt *(pages 73-83),* provides the foundation for much of what is known about Persepolis today.

As the archaeologists cleared the ashes and debris from Persepolis's Terrace, the raised stone platform on which the citadel was built, they made a spectacular find: One of the most majestic sights of Persepolis was a monumental ceremonial staircase, still standing after some 2,500 years. Leading up to the northern entrance of the Apadana, it was adorned with relief sculptures of tribute-bearing subjects. The staircase, however, was badly eroded, and the reliefs themselves had been despoiled by generations of souvenir hunters and vandals. Now, clearing the earth mounded up against the building's eastern facade, Herzfeld and his diggers discovered another gigantic stairway, a mirror image of the first. The only difference was that the surrounding soil had kept the reliefs in pristine condition, almost as the sculptors had left them 2,400 years before.

The great stairways' carvings form the greatest surviving gallery of Achaemenid art. The world portrayed by them is resolutely masculine: Of more than 3,000 figures represented, not one is female, with the exception of a leashed lioness who is being delivered by a representative from the province of Elam. The message underlying all the processions of bearded courtiers and of tribute-bearing subjects from distant lands is equally unvarying. In the words of the 19th-century British statesman and student of Persia, George Lord Curzon, "everything is devoted, with unashamed repetition, to a single purpose, the delineation of majesty in its most imperial guise."

Schmidt arrived in 1935 to continue Herzfeld's efforts, and with the advantage of a biplane at his disposal—presented to him by his wife for the use of the excavating team—the new director set to work both surveying from the skies *(pages 37-45)* and delving into the ground. He removed the detritus from a splendid chamber, slightly larger than the Apadana, where amid a forest of 100 columns, the king may have entertained or perhaps sat in state. The vast edifice was separated from the Apadana by a courtyard, which had been cleared by Herzfeld, and was named the Throne Hall by Schmidt. Later, recognizing that this function could also be attributed to the Apadana, it became known as the Hall of 100 Columns. These two impressive state rooms, both almost perfect squares, were in buildings backed by a mazelike warren of treasuries, storerooms, and residential buildings, of which little more than foundations now remain.

Both Herzfeld and Schmidt were convinced that one of these ancillary structures was the Harem of Xerxes I, the son of Darius I and his successor, known in the biblical book Esther as Ahasuerus, Esther's royal husband, who spared the lives of the Jews in Persia. Xerxes had erected most of the striking, monumental buildings at Persepolis, including his residential palace. The so-called Harem stood next door to the palace. It included 22 small two- to three-room apartments that could house a number of women and their young children. This floor plan was in fact the major factor that led Herzfeld, under whose direction the ruin was excavated and restored, to conclude that the structure had been the Harem.

At the core of the building was a stately hall and portico that opened to a courtyard. Huge reliefs adorn the four doorways to this hall. One set shows Xerxes entering the hall. While Herzfeld believed the purpose of the king's arrival would have been to visit his wives in their residence, this idea is disputed by many scholars today. Noting that neither jewelry nor other personal items had turned up in the excavation of the so-called Harem, they now think that the building may have consisted simply of a group of storerooms supplementing the adjacent Treasury, which would be excavated by Schmidt between 1935 and 1938.

Among the numerous artifacts uncovered at Persepolis were weapons, domestic utensils, additional royal inscriptions, and a pair of large stone reliefs of the king holding audience. More than 100 clay

German architect Friedrich Krefter of the Oriental Institute holds up one of the metal foundation tablets of the Apadana, the audience hall at Persepolis that he unearthed in 1933. Discovered in the northeast and southeast corners of the main portion of the structure, the tablets were encased in two limestone boxes. Each box contained two 13-inch-square tablets, one gold (right) *and one silver. Inscribed alike in Old Persian, Elamite, and Babylonian, the plaques identify Darius I as the builder of the Apadana.*

100

tablets inscribed in Elamite also came to light; most offered details of disbursements from the Treasury, including some to workers involved in the construction of Persepolis.

Although Persepolis was intended as a celebration of Achaemenid glory, the monumental complex that survives is located in an isolated spot on a walled terrace. It could only have been approached by one great stairway, whose broad, wide steps were shallow enough for a man and horse to mount. This has led to the notion that the city may have been more ceremonial than residential. Many observers have long considered the processions of gift bearers adorning the Apadana staircases as a literal representation of an annual event. The reliefs show, they argue, that the Apadana was intended, among other things, as a dramatic setting for the king to receive representatives of his subject peoples, perhaps at the New Year's festival, a high point of the Achaemenid year. But at least one scholar, Margaret Cool Root, an art historian at the University of Michigan, argues that the carvings showing the tribute bearers may represent only the abstract idea of empire, not an actual ceremony.

Whatever their interpretation, the dazzling reliefs, together with the rest of Persepolis's monumental architecture, seem out of place in an environment isolated from other habitation. So scholars began to conceive of Persepolis as a place similar to the Acropolis of Athens, the ceremonial heart of a much larger metropolis, yet to be discovered outside its walls. Tantalizing data that seemed to support this speculation surfaced in 1937 when Schmidt's aerial survey distinguished 400 features of the surrounding plain indicating earlier human settlement. Then in the 1960s epigraphist Richard Hallock of the University of Chicago, translating some 2,000 Elamite tablets found in the Persepolis fortifications, learned that they contained references to many villages and towns nearby.

Schmidt had intended to follow his aerial overviews with a

ground survey, but World War II cut short his plans. Louis vanden Berghe took up the task in the 1950s, and in 1967 a graduate student, an American named William Sumner, arrived on the scene with an impressive plan for his doctoral dissertation in archaeology from the University of Pennsylvania. Sumner would survey the whole valley below the Persepolis Terrace. Having served for 12 years as a naval officer, several of them stationed in Iran, he had become interested in the country's history and archaeology. (He also discovered the ancient Elamite city of Anshan and eventually became director of the Oriental Institute of the University of Chicago.)

In the course of his ground survey of the plain, Sumner found traces of irrigation works indicating that canals in Achaemenid times had watered the land, taking off from a river flowing from a gorge in the mountains 40 miles upstream. This meant that the area could well have supported a considerable population, estimated by Sumner to be as high as 44,000 souls. And indeed throughout the plain lay the remains of buried buildings; Sumner identified 39 places of habi-

While four Achaemenid kings—Xerxes I, Darius I and II, and Artaxerxes I—had their tombs cut into the cliff face at Naqsh-i Rustam, only Darius I's, seen on the right in the photo above, is identified by inscriptions. Tombs thought to be those of Artaxerxes II and III and Darius III are located at Persepolis. Each cross-shaped facade is over 75 feet high and 60 feet wide. The reliefs below the tombs were added in the third century AD by Sassanian kings. Darius I's crypt (right) contains three chambers, each with three burial cists. When explored by the Oriental Institute in the 1930s the tomb was empty, offering no clue as to who had been interred beside the Great King.

tation. He also uncovered a road connecting Persepolis with Susa. Less than two miles from the citadel, Sumner made a discovery that seemed to demonstrate what until then had been mere speculation: He located a large Achaemenid city, a nucleus town, surrounded by a community of large estates. He concluded that this was the city known in the Persepolis tablets as Matezzis, which Hallock and Sumner described as a large urban center that supported construction workers at Persepolis, supplying them with food, materials, and other services. "When Darius ordered the construction of Persepolis," Sumner writes, "Matezzis suddenly became a boom town, host to hundreds of foreign workers, brought in with their families for the great project."

By the mid-1990s, there had been no excavation of Matezzis, but presumably this was the city of Persepolis described by historians of Alexander as the richest city of Asia; the Terrace would have been its ceremonial center. In its heyday the city was seen as an abiding monument to Darius. His successor, Xerxes I, was at pains to stress, in the inscriptions that he left in the citadel, that he was continuing his predecessor's work, proclaiming: "What had been built by my father, I protected, and other buildings I added."

In dealing with his vassal states, however, Xerxes would prove less adept at fostering the paternal inheritance. Having mounted the

throne in peace around the age of 35 upon his father's death in 486 BC, he was at once confronted by major revolts, first in Egypt and then in Babylon. In putting down the rebellions, Xerxes demonstrated all of his father's ruthless energy, but considerably less of the magnanimity in victory that had been one of Darius's most attractive traits. Egypt, for example, according to Herodotus, was reduced "to a condition of worst servitude than it had ever been in the previous reign." In addition, Xerxes appears to have been less tolerant in religious matters than his father, asserting in one Persep-

"We must not forget that monuments are like sick people; there is no treatment that is the right one for everybody; one and the same medicine cannot be administered to all patients alike, even if they are suffering from the same illness." Giuseppe Tucci, president of the Italian Institute of the Middle and Far East (IsMEO), had chosen his analogy well. Invited by Iranian authorities in 1964 to conserve the royal city of Persepolis, the IsMEO crew, led by Giuseppe Tilia and Ann Britt Tilia, approached the task with the dedication and skill of a group of doctors.

Caged in steel, a bull's head (above) *measuring more than seven feet tall is guided into its original position in the portico of the Hall of 100 Columns at Persepolis. At right, workers replace missing pieces of a column with stone taken from the same quarries that Darius I used 2,500 years ago.*

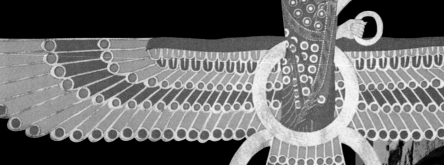

Beginning with the research of previous excavators, the husband-and-wife team undertook a campaign that would stabilize existing structures, reerect fallen columns, put reliefs back in place, and repair damaged stairways. Tucci likened the team's effort to a resurrection.

The Tilias also drew on earlier investigations to confirm that color had decorated the structures. Studies done during the excavations of the 1930s and later by researchers on a relief fragment in the Fogg Art Museum in Massachusetts convinced the archaeologists that the buildings had indeed been highlighted with blue, green, yellow, and red pigments. In a book on their work, Ann Britt Tilia remarked that "after soaking the relief section with water and by looking at it through a strong magnifying glass, we found the colors standing out brightly." The recreation above, by Giuseppe Tilia, hints at how Persepolis must have glowed under the intense rays of the Persian sun.

On a doorframe of the Council Hall (right), *a deity hovers protectively above the king, who is accompanied by attendants carrying a sunshade and a fly whisk.*

hard to imagine the background against which the treasure came to be buried: a time of rising anxiety and uncertainty as imperial power weakened, with rumors of wars and the breakdown of order leading to the final, panicky moment of concealment as raiders or invaders threatened. While no one knows precisely when the treasure was buried, one possible scenario might have been during the last stages of Alexander's victory over the Persians.

The conqueror of the Persian empire was only 23 in 334 BC when he crossed the Dardanelles and confronted Persian troops on the Granicus River, which flows into the Sea of Marmara. At Granicus he crushed the opposing forces, although he was almost killed. Pressing on through Anatolia, he learned in October 333 BC that Darius was at Issus on the Syrian coast. He intercepted the Persians as they retreated to the sea and dealt their army a severe defeat. Equally damaging was the blow to the prestige of Darius, who fled the battlefield. At Gaugamela east of the Tigris River in 331 BC, the king of Persia was forced to flee once more from an engagement with Alexander, despite having the larger army. Alexander then marched unopposed into Babylon, Susa, Pasargadae, and Persepolis, which he set alight, some say out of drunkenness, and others in revenge for the Persian destruction of the Acropolis of Athens 150 years earlier.

Alexander pursued Darius east toward Ecbatana then to Rhagae, near modern Tehran. There Bessus, the ruler of the eastern province of Bactria in northern Afghanistan, murdered Darius in the summer of 330 BC, dealing the death blow to the empire of the Persians. Bessus fled through Bactria and over the Oxus River, devastating the land as he went. He was finally overtaken by Alexander's men, tried for Darius III's murder, and in the spring of 329 BC had his nose and ears cut off; he was later executed at Ecbatana.

Perhaps it was during this last wild flight of Bessus that the Oxus Treasure was hidden. But whatever the circumstances of its concealment might have been, the hoard of splendid artifacts still speaks eloquently of the waning of the Achaemenid empire—and of the rich heritage it passed on.

THE TRIBUTE OF EMPIRE

Darius I was a man to enjoy his triumphs and boast of them—and with good reason. Under this greatest of the Persian kings an empire the likes of which the world had never seen before came into existence, with subject peoples from as far away as Egypt and India journeying to his capital of Persepolis to pay obeisance to him. "I ruled over them," ran an inscription on his tomb. "They bore tribute to me; what was said to them by me, that they did."

At Persepolis, Darius commissioned a series of carved stone reliefs (completed under the rule of his son, Xerxes I) that ran imposingly along the stairways of the Apadana, or audience hall *(detail above)*. The reliefs portray different peoples who were part of Darius's empire, each group identified by its native costume. Leading animals from their homelands, the tributaries, in a reverent, stately cadence, carry valuable indigenous raw materials—balls of thread, gold dust, ivory—and precious objects, such as exquisitely wrought amphorae

and armlets, all to be offered as tribute to the king.

Some of the individuals and groups representing delegations at Persepolis form part of this essay; on the following pages their silhouetted images are coupled with artifacts from the Achaemenid Period. Although most of the objects shown were recovered in the far-flung reaches of the Persian empire and sometimes beyond, they are typical of the kinds of gifts the tribute bearers would have presented to Darius.

Exposure to the diverse styles and tastes of the realm was to influence artists of the Achaemenid Period deeply. Indeed, the Persians eagerly took inspiration from the art and architecture of all the peoples they made subject. And in their willingness to combine foreign motifs with those of their own local tradition, the Persians managed to create an imperial style that would, in turn, have an effect on artisans throughout the continents of Europe and Asia, even long after the Achaemenids had disappeared.

This gold bowl, which is similar to the one carried by a member of the Assyrian delegation below, third from left, is embellished with handles in the shape of stretching lions, a common motif in Persian art. Presented to Czar Peter the Great by the Russian governor of Siberia, it probably came from a remote Scythian tomb in that huge region.

GANDHARAN

ASSYRIAN

From a cemetery in Duvanli, Bulgaria, the silver amphora at left closely resembles the two carried by the Lydian shown below. Rearing lions form the handles, one of which doubles as a spout. The beast on the right is missing the ibex horns that still grace the other. Amphorae like this would have been used for wine at banquets.

Adorned with elegant wings, this 11-inch-high ibex functioned as the handle of a drinking vessel. The silver and gold figure incorporates several stylistic elements. The position and rendering of the animal's body is Greek, while the mask on the base combines features of two gods—the Greek Silenus and the Phoenician-Egyptian Bes.

LYDIAN

Wrought of gold and precious stones, the necklaces above found in an Achaemenid Period tomb in Susa reiterate the Persians' love of adornment. Many of the materials used—such as the gold dust carried in bottles inside baskets by the Indian at far right, below—were probably imported into the region.

PARTHIAN

Earrings inlaid with turquoise and lapis lazuli and similar in design to this pair from Susa were common during the Achaemenid Period; they were worn by both men and women. The technique of inlaying, common throughout Middle Eastern cultures, may have been derived from the Egyptians.

A milky white glass jar decorated with red and white eyes (above) lay at Babylon in the grave of an Achaemenid Period girl. Glass vessels were being manufactured in Mesopotamia as early as the mid-second millennium BC, and several fragments of glassware discovered at Persepolis may be the remains of objects imported from there.

INDIAN

117

Preserved in the frozen earth of Siberia for more than 2,000 years, this rem-
nant (above) of a horse's woolen breast
band, woven in Persia, suggests the flow
of Persian products during Achaemenid
times. Below, two Ionian tributaries at
Persepolis carry cloth and balls of thread,
perhaps silk or spun gold.

ELAMITE

IONIAN

IONIAN

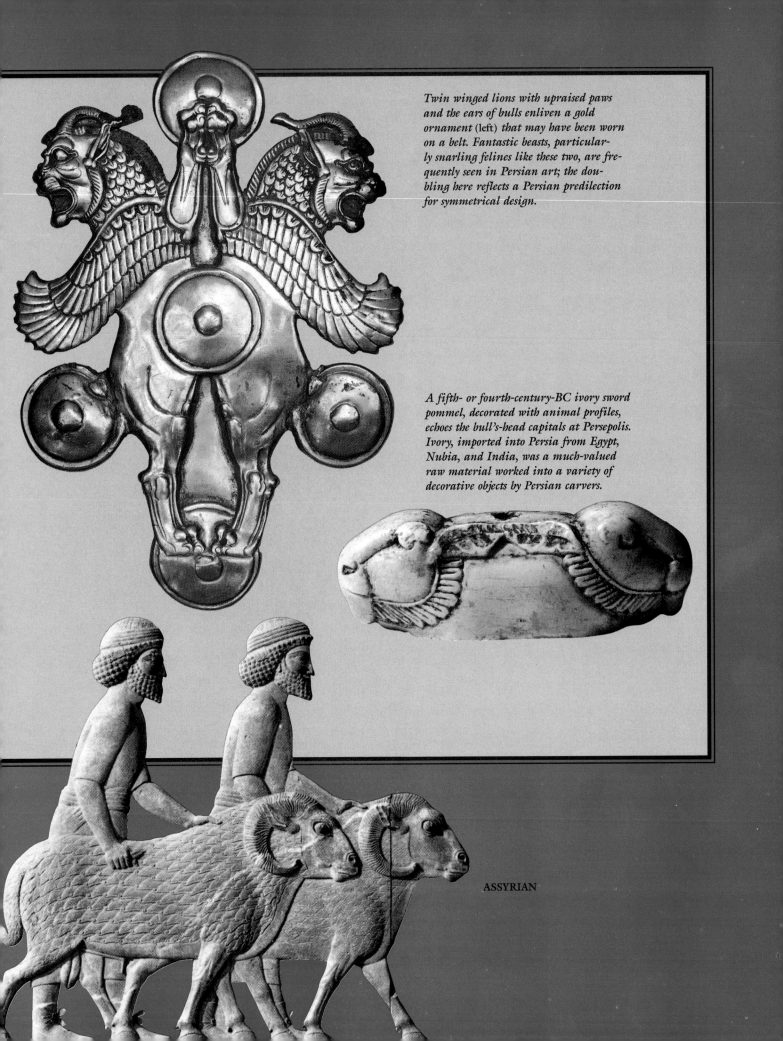

Twin winged lions with upraised paws and the ears of bulls enliven a gold ornament (left) that may have been worn on a belt. Fantastic beasts, particularly snarling felines like these two, are frequently seen in Persian art; the doubling here reflects a Persian predilection for symmetrical design.

A fifth- or fourth-century-BC ivory sword pommel, decorated with animal profiles, echoes the bull's-head capitals at Persepolis. Ivory, imported into Persia from Egypt, Nubia, and India, was a much-valued raw material worked into a variety of decorative objects by Persian carvers.

ASSYRIAN

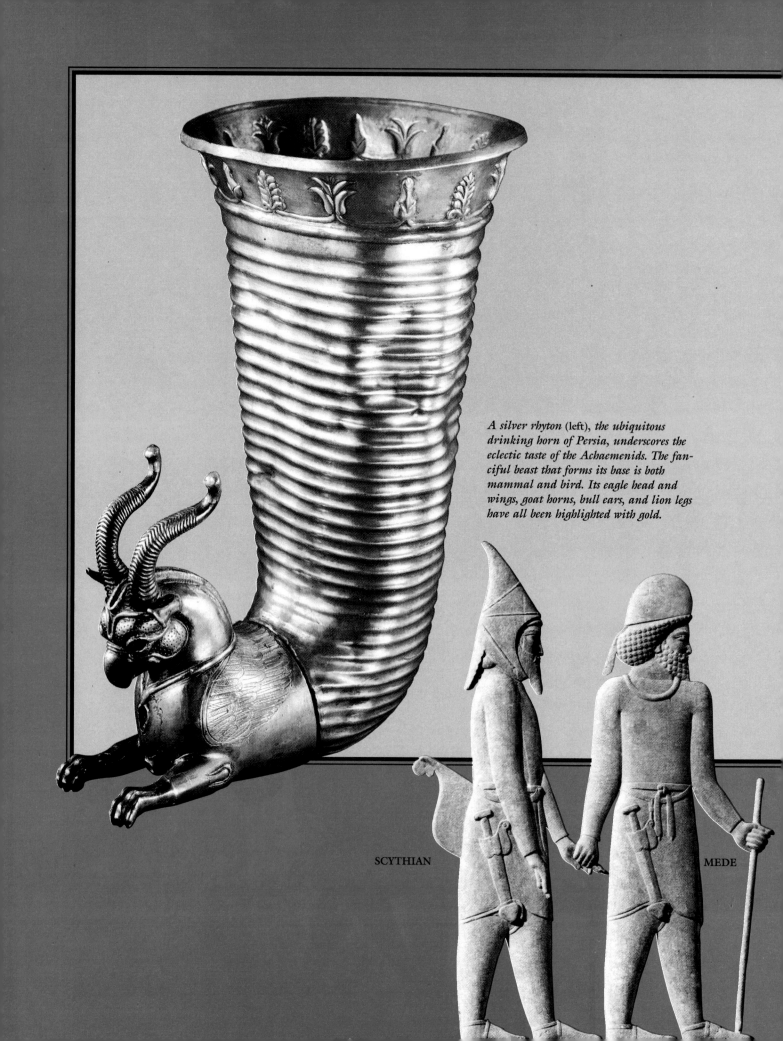

A silver rhyton (left), the ubiquitous drinking horn of Persia, underscores the eclectic taste of the Achaemenids. The fanciful beast that forms its base is both mammal and bird. Its eagle head and wings, goat horns, bull ears, and lion legs have all been highlighted with gold.

SCYTHIAN

MEDE

This gold scabbard, from the Oxus Treasure, resembles those seen dangling at the sides of the Scythian tributaries and the Median escort below. It is embossed with scenes of a royal hunt. The hunters wear Persian trousers, although their headgear echoes that worn by Assyrian kings.

The gold armlet at right—one of the most spectacular pieces of jewelry from the Oxus Treasure—terminates in griffins. Armlets were considered a prestige gift at the Persian courts, a custom obvious to the Scythian below, who carries two of them to present to the Persian king.

SCYTHIANS

THE RISE AND FALL–AND RISE– OF EMPIRES

Relic of the Sassanians—the last native dynasty to rule a Persian empire—a carved rock wall near the royal city of Bishapur honors two kings. Directly above the water channel, double rows of Shapur II's stoic nobles are depicted; to the left, but only partly visible, is another relief showing the investiture of Bahram I.

In early 1920, British soldiers led by Captain M. C. Murphy were patrolling the Syrian desert along the middle reaches of the Euphrates against hostile Arabs. In March they set up camp in the ruins of an ancient fortress high above the river near the village of Salihiyah. Poking about at the citadel's west corner, Murphy spotted something worth reporting to his commanding officer: "I discovered some ancient wall paintings in a wonderful state of preservation," Murphy wrote in a letter. "The paintings consist of life-size figures of three men, one woman, and three other figures partly obliterated. The colors are mainly reds, yellows, and black. There is also some writing which I have tried to reproduce below."

Murphy's news was sent by his colonel, together with some undeveloped photographs of the figures, to higher British authorities in Baghdad. "The paintings," the colonel noted, "are most interesting and should be seen by an expert. If your American archaeologist is still about, it would well repay him to come and see this." The scholar he was referring to was James Henry Breasted, a prominent Egyptologist who, at the time, happened to be in the Middle East as head of a University of Chicago team buying antiquities and exploring sites for possible digs in the region. Alerted to Murphy's fascinating discovery, Breasted and his colleagues set off for Salihiyah in seven British army vehicles.

123

The journey over largely roadless wastes was trying, not least for Breasted himself, who was 54 years old. The group averaged little more than 40 miles a day. There is little doubt that Breasted judged the effort worthwhile, however, as is clear from his description of what he and his party saw after reaching the crumbled fortress and making their way "over the rubbish piles commonly found in such ruins and around a jutting corner of massive masonry. Suddenly there rose before us a high wall covered with an imposing painting in many colors depicting a life-size group of eleven persons engaged in worship. It was a startling revelation of the fact that in this

A roiling cloud of sand rushes toward the ruins of Dura-Europos in this photograph taken along the western perimeter. The storm suggests how the ancient city felled by the Sassanians in the third century AD came to lie hidden until the 1920s, when excavations began. "The stone walls of Dura," wrote American archaeologist Clark Hopkins, field director of excavations from 1931 to 1935, "rose out of the desert like the bones of some long-lost, half-submerged dinosaur buried 20 and 30 feet in desert sand."

Worn steps (above) *ascend to the cult niche of Dura-Europos's Mithraeum, temple of the Romanized god Mithras, long associated with the Persian deity of justice, Mithra. Bas-reliefs of the god in Persian dress are surrounded by painted images, including two seated figures clasping scrolls and canes. The men are believed to be magi, or priests* (detail below). *Roman soldiers, who revered Mithras, probably built this Mithraeum, as they did many others throughout their empire.*

deserted stronghold we were standing in a home of ancient Syrian civilization completely lost to the western world for sixteen centuries." In fact, nearly two decades of archaeological examination would result from this first scholarly examination of the site, opening a window onto a succession of ancient societies, all heirs, in one way or another, to the Achaemenid empire.

Breasted was not the first archaeologist to visit the site. In 1912, Germans Friedrich Sarre and Ernst Herzfeld had made photos and drawings of the place, but windblown sand had concealed these murals from them. Still, they had found Greek stonework, a few fragments of paintings, and inscriptions that suggested that the city had been built by Macedonians—veterans of Alexander the Great's army—probably around 300 BC, when Persia was ruled by a dynasty of Alexander's Macedonian heirs known as the Seleucids.

The dazzling murals, Breasted determined, must be the work of Parthians, an Iranian people who wrested the old Persian realm from the Seleucids during the second century BC and for some 400 years thereafter maintained an empire that in many ways equaled that of the Romans to the west. Some of the paintings in fact reflected the Roman-Parthian competition for this region. "We saw to our surprise a small scene in which a Roman tribune was depicted at the head of his troops," Breasted reported. This officer was "engaged in the worship of what looked like three statues of Roman emperors painted on the wall." Moreover, the officer's name and rank were written next to him in Roman letters: "Julius Terentius, tribune." And before him, Breasted noted, "was the red battle flag of Roman troops," indicating the place had, at one time, been an outpost of the Romans.

Breasted also found a picture of a sacrificial scene and two goddesses on which the artist had painted a title: "The Fortunes of Dura and Palmyra." So this place was Dura, which, according to the second-century Greek historian Isidore of Charax, the Greeks called Europos. The word *dura* is a common semitic term for fortified settlements, probably a reference to the city's mighty walls. It is likely that the Greeks renamed it Europos to honor Seleucus I Nicator, founder of the Seleucid dynasty and many of its cities, who had been born in the Macedonian town of Europos.

Breasted left that day, and the soldiers covered the paintings with sand to protect them, but by 1922, when archaeologists sponsored by the French Academy came to dig there, the images had deteriorated. So rich was the site, however, the French remained in the area for two seasons. Then in 1927 a decade of excavation in Dura-Europos began under the joint auspices of the French Academy and Yale University, directed by French scholar Maurice Pillet until 1931, when American archaeologist Clark Hopkins took command.

Piecing together their finds, these scholars discovered how, on a small scale, Dura-Europos mirrored much of what had happened to the former Persian empire in the centuries after Alexander's invasion. Built by Macedonians during the reign of the Seleucid kings, seized by Parthians, intermittently occupied by Romans, the fortress town was home to followers of Persia's Zoroastrian and Mithraist faiths, worshipers of Greek and Roman gods, and Jews and Christians. Finally, it would succumb in the third century AD to the Sassanians, who repeated the conquests of the Achaemenid empire and reinvigorated Persian traditions, spreading them into the Hellenized world. Some in the old Persian world may have greeted the ideas of this new regime as a rebirth, but for Dura-Europos, the whirlwind of Sassanian conquest spelled disaster.

Alexander had envisioned a far rosier future for his empire. He had hoped for a peaceful and fruitful union of the peoples of Europe with those of the newly conquered Middle East when, in 324 BC, he compelled 80 of his top Macedonian officers to marry Persian noblewomen in a mass wedding at Susa. He may have thought their Euro-Asian progeny would unite the Greek and Persian worlds through blood ties. Although he already had a Persian wife, he took another on this grand occasion, Barsine, the oldest daughter of Persia's late king, Darius III. "The marriages were celebrated according to Persian custom," wrote Roman historian Arrian in the second century AD, when now-lost sources describing the event were still available to him. "Chairs were placed for the bridegrooms, and after the drinks, the brides came in and sat down, each by the side of her groom. [The grooms] took them by the hand and kissed them; the king began the ceremony, for all the weddings took place together."

Any notions Alexander had about the intermingling of cultures collapsed when he died. After his death in 323 BC, all but one of the officers wed that day in Susa rejected their wives. They and their troops may still have been smoldering over the sight of Alexander in Persian clothes, teaching Macedonian battle techniques to Persian officers he was training for his army. From the beginning of his

THE PERSIAN GOD WHO BATTLED EVIL

With the cult of fire at its core, the Persian religion known as Zoroastrianism burned brightly in the minds of its followers, kings as well as commoners. Beginning among agriculturists in Central Asia perhaps as early as 1700 BC and evolving in Persia over the centuries, it was adopted by the Sassanians as their state religion.

Like Christianity and Islam, both of which it foreshadowed, Zoroastrianism was founded by one man, Zoroaster. He believed that he had been chosen by Ahura Mazda, the supreme being. His god-ordained mission was to teach the truth. According to Zoroaster, Ahura Mazda is the creator of heaven and earth and light and darkness. As originator of the moral order as well, he stands at the center of nature, surrounded by a hierarchy of seven subordinate spirits. These are not so much divinities as different aspects of the one god. They are Spenta Mainyu, the Holy Spirit; Vohu Manah, Good Mind; Asha Vahishta, Universal Truth and Order; Khsharthra, Dominion; Armaiti, Benevolence; Haurvatat, Salvation; and Ameretat, Immortality.

The Holy Spirit is at war with Angra Mainyu, the Destructive Spirit—the Lie. Both, in turn, try to influence people; it is the responsibility of all to choose between them and to help others pursue "Good Thoughts, Good Words, Good Deeds." The great god will judge these individuals after death. If they elect goodness, they will enjoy a happy afterlife; if evil, their lot will be one of torment. Zoroaster carried this notion of heaven and hell a step further; he spoke of a final stage for the visible world. In this "last turn of creation," Angra Mainyu, Evil and the Lie, will be destroyed and the earth renewed, to become the paradisiacal home of the just forever.

rule, Alexander had promoted many Persians to high office. Increasingly influenced by Persia, he had adopted its customs. But instead of promoting brotherhood, his partiality toward Persians had angered the Macedonians, resulting in further divisiveness.

Alexander's successors were soon locked in an internecine battle notable for sudden, devious shifts of alliances and murderous disloyalty among men who had been comrades in arms. In 310 BC one faction did not hesitate to assassinate even Alexander's widow, Roxane, and son Alexander, a stroke that dispelled any lingering hope of an Alexandrian dynasty—along with any of chivalry or mercy.

By then, three regional rulers were established within the boundaries of Alexander's former empire, although they and others would fight among themselves for decades. One of Alexander's generals, Ptolemy, had seized Egypt, while another, Antigonus Monophthalmus, meaning the "One-Eyed," laid claim to the Macedonian throne itself and soon controlled a large part of Anatolia and Syria. The third was Seleucus—eventually known as Seleucus I Nicator, or the "Conqueror"—a tough, highly effective soldier and yet, for his time and rank, atypically lenient as husband, father, and monarch.

The face of Seleucus, as seen on coins of the period, is distinguished by a strong nose and chin and deep-set eyes; he was as powerfully handsome as Alexander. Seleucus had commanded the infantry during Alexander's campaign in India from 327 to 325 BC. In 321 BC, Seleucus became satrap of Babylonia. When his erstwhile ally, Antigonus, demanded an accounting of the satrapy's incomes, Seleucus refused to comply. Lacking sufficient forces to make a stand, he fled to Egypt, but he returned in 312 BC with an army borrowed from Ptolemy. Helped by the local goodwill he had engendered during his tenure as satrap, he drubbed Antigonus's occupation force.

The grateful Babylonians honored the victor's entry into their city on the first of the month of Nisan—or April 3, 311 BC—by declaring that day the beginning of a new era, the Seleucid age, thus formally marking the founding of the Seleucid empire on the Babylonian calendar; the Macedonian calendar already had declared the beginning of this era on October 1, 312 BC. Soon Seleucus set about expanding his realm to the east, in an attempt to recover land won by Alexander and subsequently lost. He first defeated his Bactrian adversaries, and the next year he invaded northern India. There he discovered that the numerous principalities with small armies he had helped Alexander to conquer were no more; they had been replaced

by a powerful, unified state led by the great Indian empire builder Chandragupta Maurya. Seleucus wisely decided to make a treaty. He yielded Macedonian territorial claims in the Indus Valley, and as part of the compensation for having done so, he received from Chandragupta no fewer than 500 trained fighting elephants.

A sight rarely seen in the Mediterranean world, the elephants proved an invaluable asset when Seleucus turned his military attention westward to Syria and beyond. In an alliance with the kings of Macedon and Thrace, Seleucus and his elephants confronted Antigonus Monophthalmus at the Battle of Ipsus in northern Syria in 301 BC. The array of huge, foreign, foul-smelling, trumpeting beasts apparently had a devastating impact on enemy morale. As the forces of Antigonus—including his son Demetrius—fled the field, he himself was killed. With that victory Seleucus established an empire that reached from the boundaries of India in the east to the borders of Anatolia in the west, most of what the Achaemenids, and later Alexander, had ruled.

For a foreigner, Seleucus enjoyed an advantage that put him in good stead with the Persians. It was he, alone among the 80 Macedonian officers in the mass wedding at Susa, who had not rejected his wife Apame, daughter of Spitamenes, the overlord of Bactria. Seleucus may have kept her because he did not wish to deal her such a devastating insult, or because he genuinely loved her. But it may also have been because he believed her pedigree would enhance the authority of their dynastic heirs.

Workers push excavation carts down the center of Dura-Europos's Market Street in this 1930s picture (actually two photos imperfectly spliced for a broader view). The street's shops—whose ruins can be seen here—were part of the agora, or marketplace, built around 300 BC by the Seleucids, then enlarged some 200 years later after the Parthians captured the city.

A year after defeating Antigonus in 301 BC, Seleucus I founded a new city in Syria, Antioch-on-the-Orontes, named after his father; in the following decade it would become his capital. Part of his agenda was to assert his claim to Syria, the southern portion of which was occupied by his former allies, the Ptolemies of Egypt. To do so he engaged in one of those convoluted political maneuvers that characterized the Macedonians' endless grappling. Turning to none other than

Demetrius—the son of Antigonus the One-Eyed, whom he had defeated and killed in battle—he asked for the hand of the king's famously beautiful daughter Stratonice.

Demetrius assented, and in 298 BC, Seleucus and Stratonice were joined as husband and wife in a splendid wedding at Rhosus in Syria. Intended to mark the birth of an alliance between Seleucus and Demetrius, the marriage in fact gave rise to a scandal—or so the ancient accounts go. Crown Prince Antiochus I, Seleucus's son by Apame and the half-Macedonian, half-Bactrian heir to the Seleucid throne, grew deathly ill with a malady doctors could not diagnose. According to the second-century-AD Roman historian Appian, the famous Greek physician Erasistratos diagnosed the young man's illness as psychosomatic. Studying the prince's responses to those who entered his sickroom, he had noticed that whenever his stepmother appeared, he began to stammer, blush, sweat, and grow pale. Antiochus's secret was out: He had fallen madly in love with Stratonice. The impossibility of attaining his desires, and the need to repress them, had made him extremely ill.

Antiochus was fortunate; another king might have had such a rival killed. Seleucus instead divorced Stratonice and gave her to Antiochus on the advice of the doctor, and perhaps goaded by Apame, who may not have been too pleased about sharing her husband with

Drinking cup in hand, club resting by his feet, a life-size Heracles lounges on a lion skin beside the Silk Road at Behistun. A protective canopy casts a shadow across a corner of the Seleucid rock carving, which has been dated 148 BC by a Greek inscription found behind it.

the young beauty. Furthermore, Seleucus named Antiochus coregent in command of the satrapies east of the Tigris.

It was long believed that Seleucus pursued Alexander's one-time goal of double rule: Persian officials working alongside Greeks. A scholar who checked lists of bureaucrats, however, indicates that even after two generations of Seleucid control less than 3 percent of ordinary government officials, such as clerks, accountants, and others below the executive level, were locals. Indeed, Persians found most doors tightly shut to them. They almost never gained admission to the gymnasia, which were as much exclusive clubs as places to bathe and exercise, and public athletic contests usually admitted only Greek competitors.

Perhaps because there was always a threat of an insurrection, Seleucus and his successors planted Greek colonists in newly constructed cities throughout the empire to preserve Greek power. Dura-Europos was one example, and there were many others as well, including

Excavators in the 1930s uncover a barrel-vault tomb among the Parthian-level ruins of Seleucia-on-the-Tigris, the Seleucid capital that first came under Parthian influence in the second century BC. Parthian artifacts found here include the second-century-AD marble woman reclining below, nude but for a necklace and a pair of sandals.

130

at least 11 Seleucias—named after Seleucus or his dynasty—in Anatolia, Syria, Mesopotamia, and Iran. Constructed according to Greek city plans, these sat like islands of Hellenistic culture in an alien sea.

Protected by the Seleucid king and his army, such cities flourished. Seleucia-on-the-Tigris, built near Babylon, became the eastern capital, probably in a deliberate attempt to reduce the power of Babylon. If that is what was intended, the scheme worked: A number of Babylonians, seeking advancement, joined the Greek colonists in settling there, to the distress of other Babylonians whose age-old city began to decline as the new center's population grew to 600,000.

The river no longer flowed beside Seleucia-on-the-Tigris when an expedition under the aegis of the University of Michigan began digging there in 1927, although aerial photographs confirmed that it had indeed done so. During the subsequent decade of excavations, the archaeologists learned that the city had been carefully planned. The residential area stood at the center, edged by two great transportation arteries. The main road through the city lay to the south; across this avenue were the marketplace and civic buildings. To the north was the royal canal with its flow of traffic between the Euphrates and the Tigris Rivers, and beyond the canal was the temple and palace district. Digging through three occupation levels revealed the original Seleucid city with its Hellenistic buildings laid out in a rectangular grid; in the next layer up, marking the onset of Parthian rule, the planning was less rigid, and Middle Eastern features were introduced; the top layer, representing the peak of Parthian power, displayed a preponderance of these oriental elements, and an almost complete breakdown of the original Hellenistic structure.

The ruins of Susa reveal a similar pattern. Still a major center in Seleucid times, the city was renamed Seleucia of Eulaios. Known as a hub of international trade, Susa was also an administrative center where coins were minted for the Seleucid kings. Although little remains of its Greek-era buildings today, surviving inscriptions on stone refer to such typically Greek structures as the gymnasium and indicate that Greek gods, particularly Artemis and Apollo, were worshiped in the city. Its Macedonian ruling class may have lived in the large area of the city excavated by French archaeologist Roman Ghirshman from 1946 to 1967; his digging laid bare a network of perpendicular streets, once lined with huge houses adorned with Greek friezes.

131

As elsewhere in the Seleucid empire, few Susians were involved in the city's administration. The center of Elamite language and culture had shifted to the mountains to the east, an area that became known as Elymais, and maintained commercial relations with Susa.

With its capital so far to the west, the Seleucid kings were unable to keep control of the regions on the Iranian Plateau. These provinces became effectively independent of the empire either under Greek rulers, as was the case in Bactria, or under the control of local kings, as in Persis. Strong Seleucid monarchs such as Antiochus III reestablished their authority over local kings, but in general the provinces were not interfered with by the Seleucids. Most of the information about this region comes from coins, and there seems to be a striking dearth of Seleucid coins in Persis compared with the multitude dug up in other provinces.

Seleucus ruled until 281 BC, when he was assassinated by a Ptolemy, but not before he had annexed the Thracian Peninsula and thereby established control of the Dardanelles, leading to the Aegean Sea. Then in 190 BC a Roman army, dispatched by a Senate convinced that the Seleucids had designs on Europe, marched into Lydia in western Anatolia. They thrashed a force sent by Antiochus III, the sixth in the Seleucid line of kings, thereby ending the Seleucid presence in Europe and Asia Minor.

Two decades later the Seleucid decline was hastened by a younger son of Antiochus III, known as Antiochus IV Epiphanes, meaning "famous." He was determined to forcibly Hellenize those Middle Easterners who, after more than a century of Seleucid rule, still did not fully embrace Greek ways. His attention was drawn to Judah, to which Antiochus III had granted a considerable amount of self-rule. Imposing Greek gods and rituals in this part of his domain would require stamping out, or at least reducing, the faith of a fiercely independent people dedicated to a monotheistic religion. The dramatic story of the clash between Antiochus and the Jews is told in the First Book of Maccabees, which is part of the collection of Jewish historical documents that were not included in the Old Testament and are known as the Apocrypha.

In 174 BC, Antiochus first earned the enmity of devout Jews by appointing Jason to the high priesthood because he offered to increase the taxes of Judah. Two years later Menelaus, a man widely considered unqualified for the position, promised even higher taxes and was given that office. Menelaus's enemies threw him out after three years. Furious, Antiochus stormed Jerusalem in 168 BC, stationing troops in the city and enraging the Jews with acts that were in deliberate violation of their religious practices. He halted the daily rites of sacrifice to Judaism's one god and desecrated the Temple's altar, introducing into the sanctuary the worship of a pagan deity.

Similar outrages were visited on the villages of Judah, including Modein, home to a priest named Mattathias of the Hasmonean family and his five strapping sons. Mattathias was unable to restrain his anger. He killed a Jew who was preparing to sacrifice to Ba'al—and the Seleucid officer who had been sent to oversee the proceedings. Mattathias and his sons escaped to the hills, where they launched a guerrilla campaign that became a war of independence.

One of the brothers, Judas, proved a brilliant military leader. He took the surname Maccabee, based on the Aramaic word *maqqabah,* for "hammer." In the Apocryphal account, Judas and his small army engaged the superior forces of the king in a series of battles; the Jews allegedly fought valiantly, winning a string of small military victories but without resolving the issue of religious autonomy. The turning point came with the death of Antiochus in November of 164 BC. Judas then led his troops into Jerusalem itself, tore down the pagan altar, built a new one, and purified the Temple. Then, exactly three years after the desecration of the Temple, Judas and his followers began an eight-day festival of rededication, celebrated by Jews annually since then as Hanukkah.

Judah retained its autonomy under a succession of Seleucid kings who reigned for almost 100 years. By the beginning of the first century BC, however, their once-great empire had lost all its territory east of the Euphrates to a dynasty known as the Parthians, and it had shrunk to a small state in Syria and eastern Cilicia.

Although ancient sources mentioned the Parthians, not much was known about them in the West for centuries after their own demise. In the second century AD the Roman historian Justin remarked on their equestrian way of life: "On horses they go to war, to banquets, to public and private tasks, and on them they travel, stay still, do business and chat." They were said to have been a Scythian people who had moved into Parthia, a province in northeast Iran, in

A Hellenistic helmet protects the head of a warrior from Nysa, capital of the Parthian homeland, located near Ashkhabad, Turkmenistan. Archaeologists discovered the second-century-BC painted-clay head in a room not far from Nysa's monumental Square Hall in the 1980s.

the early third century BC, during the Seleucid period. Accounts differ, but apparently a Parthian named Arsaces, a man "of undisputed bravery," according to Justin, led an uprising sometime after 250 BC and overthrew the Seleucid satrap. When Seleucus II tried to regain his province in 228 BC, he was defeated by Arsaces, whose military feats in the area were establishing what would be the Arsacid dynasty.

Parthian coins would offer modern scholars clues to events, particularly the royal succession. They showed that Arsaces was followed by a line of competent warrior-kings who expanded the Parthian domain. The outstanding Parthian military leader, however, was Mithradates I, who ruled from 171 to 138 BC. Mithradates, considered the founder of the Parthian empire, established cities and expanded the Parthian realm from Babylonia to Bactria, at the expense of the Seleucids and semi-independent regions such as Bactria and Persis. Among the settlements he established was a huge hilltop fortress town at Nysa, near modern Ashkhabad in Turkmenistan east of the Caspian Sea.

"Old Nysa," as the ancient site is called by scholars, was excavated from 1948 to 1961 by Soviet archaeologists, who identified it by an inscribed potsherd they found there as the town of Mithradatkert, probably named after Mithradates. This great citadel was enclosed by imposing walls that rose to more than 80 feet in height and were 16 feet thick. Any would-be attacker would have had to ascend a gradually rising ramp along the outer perimeter of the defenses, the only possible means of entry, and risk a hail of arrows from above.

As the ruins of a palace, temples, and several other public edifices indicated to the archaeologists, Nysa's builders had drawn on various architectural and decorative styles. They used, for example, both Doric and Corinthian columns in some rooms. Boldly, they constructed roofs that spanned 55 feet, apparently with no internal support. Among the most compelling discoveries at Nysa was a stunning collection of precious objects sealed in a building the excavators called the Square Hall. This treasure included some 60 ivory drinking horns, or rhyta, carved with figures that are classically Greek in some instances and in the oriental mode in others, a clear expression of the cultural diversity that characterized Parthian art and life at this juncture.

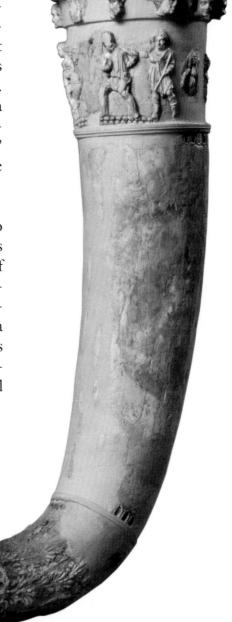

The success of Mithradates is evident in the fact that by 140 BC the royal die cutters at Seleucia-on-the-Tigris, the eastern Seleucid capital, were turning out coins bearing his profile. There he established a precedent that undoubtedly assisted Parthian rule. He left the Greek residents of the city at peace. Thereafter the Parthians made a practice of letting conquered Seleucid cities remain Greek. Furthermore, the wily Mithradates I no doubt earned himself a measure of goodwill among his new subjects by having himself designated on coins as the "Philhellene," or "Lover of things Greek." Eventually the Parthians established their capital at Ctesiphon, on the opposite bank of the river from Seleucia-on-the-Tigris.

Only in the last 100 years or so have archaeological discoveries turned up hard facts about the cultural character and achievement of the Parthians. Between 1903 and 1914, for instance, German archaeologist Ernest Walter Andrae excavated—atop the partially uncovered ruins of the much older Assyrian capital of Assur—part of a Parthian metropolis that may have been called Labbana. Andrae's painstaking care enabled him to come up with not only the basic layouts of Labbana's temples, homes, and grand palaces but also crucial details of Parthian engineering. Most important of the latter was the secret that made possible the immense, barrel-vaulted rooms known as iwans *(page 138),* a breakthrough achieved with a mortar prepared from local gypsum that bonded so quickly the bricks were held in place almost as soon as they were laid. The workers were thus able to dispense with supportive scaffolding as they placed the bricks in the semicircular pattern that created the great vaulted ceilings. The palace at Labbana is characterized by a central rectangular courtyard, with a huge iwan dominating each of its four sides.

On the Silk Road 37 miles northwest of Assur was the trading city of Hatra, where many iwans have also been found. Hatra, a vassal city of the Parthians, managed to withstand the might of Rome. In AD 117, Trajan tried unsuccessfully to conquer Hatra, and in AD 198 and the following year as well, Septimus Severus was unable to pierce its defenses. These consisted of an almost circular four-mile-long set of two walls with a ditch, 60 to 100 feet wide, outside both. The city was first surveyed by Andrae in 1908; extensive excavations, however, would not begin until much later, in 1951, when they were directed by Iraqi archaeologist Fuad Safar.

If a city's strength reflects its status, Hatra must have been among the most important of the oasis trading centers with its many springs. Among the public buildings that once stood at the city's center was the Temple of Shamash, the sun god. It was composed of two large iwans, 45 by 90 feet, each flanked by two smaller ones. By Andrae's estimate, the ceilings of the two large iwans had soared 60 feet above the floor. The arches and lintels were adorned with friezes, showing in high relief rows of human heads and busts of deities. Stone statues of humans and eagles were also uncovered.

The use of iwans at Labbana, Hatra, and other sites was not limited to palaces and temples but occurred widely in smaller public buildings and private houses. Serving as living rooms for entertaining friends, iwans provided shade in the summer and an opening for the circulation of air.

Some fascinating Parthian remains turned up at some distance from major cities or trade centers. In 1935 at the village of Shami in southwestern Iran about 50 miles

east of Susa, a group of seminomadic Lurs, under official orders to settle down permanently, were constructing their half-below-ground huts on the government-assigned site, a high hillside. While they were making trenches for the footings of their headman's abode, a spade clinked against something metallic. It was a life-size bronze statue of a man *(page 140)*, buried with smaller fragments of bronze and marble statuary. The district administrator was summoned to inspect the location and carry the finds back to his headquarters. He was still awaiting instructions from his superiors in Tehran six months later, when Aurel Stein, a British orientalist, came through on a trek across western Iran. At 73, the scholarly adventurer had spent a lifetime exploring the ruins of Central Asia, India, and Iran.

On viewing what he called a "remarkable archaeological find," Stein knew that, as he later wrote, "it was manifestly important to secure as exact a record as I could, particularly as the sculptures clearly dated from Parthian times, the least known period in the history of Iranian art." The standing male figure was hollow, probably cast by the lost-wax method. The head was found separate from the body. When its pieces were assembled, the statue measured 6 feet 4 inches tall and 26 inches across the shoulders.

Although the district administrator had left word that there be no more digging at Shami, Stein worried about antiques dealers beating him to the site, so he decided to head there as soon as possible. With an escort of 10 gendarmes provided by the governor of Fars province at the outset of his trip, Stein made the three-day midwinter journey into the rugged mountains by mule, his preferred mode of travel for rough country—far better, he maintained, than donkey or camel. "It was due to the remarkable qualities of these mules that even the winter rains did not seriously impede our progress," he declared, "especially amidst slippery limestone hills."

At Shami, Stein was pleased to see no sign that anyone had violated the proscription against digging. When laborers cleared the site of a five-foot-deep covering of earth, he discovered that a structure that had stood there "had been completely wrecked and burned" centuries earlier, as indicated by the "masses of ashes and charred wood." A three-foot-high brick altar and the stone bases for at least a dozen statues, such as the one that had been recovered, told him the building apparently had been a shrine or cult center. He found pieces of enough images to account for about 10 statues. Examining the structure's foundation stones, Stein calculated that its

Bedecked in flowing gown, headdress, and jewels, a noblewoman of Hatra reflects Parthian fashions of the second century AD. Archaeologists have gleaned knowledge about Parthian jewelry from statues such as this one as well as from unearthed examples. Those pieces include the third-century-AD earring from Hatra shown at top left, made of gold and spinel (a rubylike gem), and the first- or second-century-AD gold-and-pearl earring from Seleucia, inset with an oval garnet.

SOARING IWANS AND MAJESTIC DOMES OF THE PARTHIANS AND SASSANIANS

Awed by the Taq-i Kisra's enormity, long-ago visitors to the beautiful palace at Ctesiphon swore it seemed the work of genies. The Sassanian structure, with its towering vaults, owed more to Parthian architects, however, than magical beings.

In palaces, temples, and homes, Parthians erected iwans, vaulted rooms with one open side that usually led to a courtyard. Builders could span such spaces without centering or supportive columns. Techniques included laying a vault in sloping half-circles back to front using fast-bonding mortar. Columns appear as decorative elements on the iwans' stucco facades.

Sassanians offered their own innovations, including the squinch. This small supportive structure bridged adjacent walls at the corner, allowing builders to crown a square room with a dome. Sassanian domes and iwans influenced European Romanesque architecture.

The 115-foot-high iwan of the Sassanian palace Taq-i Kisra is seen below in the 1880s, just before half the facade fell. Taq-i Kisra resembles the Parthian palace of Assur, reconstructed above.

On a mountaintop not far from modern-day Firuzabad, goats rest among the crumbling third-century-AD ruins of Ardashir I's palace. The first Sassanian king built his palace with its iwans and domes near the city he called the Glory of Ardashir.

A jagged hole exposes the interior of the dome at the third-century-AD fortified palace of Qaleh-i Dukhtar to daylight. The squinches—seen on either side of the small arched niche at the photo's center—cupping the corners of the room may be the earliest example of this Sassanian device for setting a dome atop a square room.

Through Persian eyes, the conflict with Rome was not simply a matter of troops swooping down on innocent citizens. According to Shapur, the first clash of the two powers—when Roman Emperor Gordian III raised "a force from the Goth and German realms and marched against the Empire of Iran and against us"—was purely defensive on his part. Then, in AD 244, on the border of Babylonia, "a great frontal battle took place, and the Roman leader was killed and the Roman force was destroyed." Proclaiming Philip the Arab their leader, or caesar, they were willing to pay the Sassanians 500,000 denarii, the standard Roman coin, to buy peace. An agreement seems to have been made, which Shapur assumed gave the Sassanians carte blanche in Armenia—once ruled by Parthia, but now under Roman protection—but Shapur accused the Romans of betraying the agreement. "Caesar lied again," he reports. Rome, it seems, had given the heir to the Armenian throne, Tiridates III, refuge after Shapur had caused the death of Tiridates' father. In retaliation, the Sassanians took the offensive in AD 256 and at Barbalissos on the Euphrates allegedly "annihilated a Roman force of 60,000."

Shapur was determined to drive the Romans out of Syria, and

A Sassanian king thought to be Khosrow II (AD 590-628) slays a leaping wild boar (above, center) *from a boat; he is accompanied by a large entourage, including a second vessel filled with harp-playing musicians* (detail at right, top). *This rock relief of a royal hunt appears in the great grotto at Taq-i Bustan and is rich in details, from the pattern of the monarch's clothing to the swirling water and fish depicted just below him* (detail at right, bottom). *Modern grafitti mar the masterpiece.*

A cave in the vicinity may have been the king's
held a lifelike statue of Shapur carved from a single st:
26 feet high, it now lies on its back *(page 149)*, possibl
by an earthquake. An Islamic observer in the 14th cei
that some people believed it represented "a real man v
turned to stone."

Like their predeces
nians sought to u
peoples of their expanded domain, and religion was on
they chose to accomplish this. Shapur I showed an int<
religion and seems to have been open to new ideas.
listened to the preachings of the founder of Manichaei:
combined the teachings of Zoroaster, Jesus, and Bud
tually Shapur returned to the traditional Zoroastrian i
(pages 126-127). His successors suppressed other fai
among the instigators of this intolerance was the high

Evidence of Kartir's religious stance was disc
19th century when scholars translated an unusual Sas
tion that had been added to the relief of Shapur at N:
It boasted not of royal deeds but of those of the priest
scription revealed him to be a zealot who reveled in h
of Christians, Jews, Manichaeans, and Buddhists, ani
iron fist to bring his fellow Zoroastrians into strict or
the death of Shapur I, for instance, Kartir was amon
mental in having Mani thrown into prison, where he c
his career under Shapur, Kartir rose from junior priest
caste-rigid Sassanian society under the aegis of
Bahrams I and II, who followed Shapur I. Kartir's im:
stone behind that of Shapur.

Throughout Sassanian history, the tides of reli
shifted with the ascension of each new king, the ch:
matter of politics as of faith. Shapur II, who ruled fr
379, persecuted Christians once their religion had be
his enemies, the Romans, but the policy was apparen
lived, for subsequent Sassanian monarchs, seeking
Rome, married Christians and appointed Christian o

The pragmatism evident in the Sassanian approach t
no doubt, also a guiding force in their economic po

he attacked Dura-Europos, once under Parthian sway
and now taken over by the Romans. Vivid evidence
of this attack would come to light 17 centuries later,
in November 1932, as American archaeologist Clark
Hopkins and his team from Yale University and the
French Academy explored the ruins of the city. They
were gathered before an interior wall of a building
they had been excavating with special care, sensing
that the original plaster might still be intact. "I clearly remember when the [last] foot of fill dirt still covering the back wall was undercut and fell away,"
Hopkins recalled, "exposing the most amazing succession of paintings! Whole scenes, figures, and objects burst into view, brilliant in color, magnificent in
the sunshine." Study revealed that these were part of
a third-century-AD synagogue covered with scenes
from the Old Testament.

The extraordinary condition of the paintings,
archaeologists later decided, could be largely credit-
ed to the last-ditch defenses of the Romans. Know-
ing that the Sassanians were traveling toward Dura-
Europos, the Romans occupying the city had hurried to fortify the
outer wall. They had filled the street and buildings behind it with
dirt. Thus the synagogue, enlarged and refurbished only 20 years before, was buried to the rafters.

While these measures preserved the paintings, they proved
useless against the onslaught, and Dura-Europos fell. Archaeologists
would find a silent vignette of the contest in a tunnel beneath one of
the fortress walls. On one side lay the remains of a score of armed
Roman soldiers; confronting them was the skeleton of one lone Persian warrior with a sword. The synagogue was left undisturbed for
nearly 17 centuries, its paintings protected by the dry desert sands.

Shapur mentions Dura-Europos in his inscriptions as one of
"a total of 37 towns" that his army "burned, ruined, pillaged." His
most astonishing victory over the Romans, near Edessa three years
later, around AD 259, was recalled in a 25-foot-high rock relief showing two Roman emperors paying homage to him, one on bended
knee. For at Edessa he not only had defeated a Roman army of some
70,000 but, in a deed almost unique in history, had captured a Roman emperor, Valerian, alive. "We made prisoner ourselves with our

own hands Valerian Caesar and the others," a commemorative inscription boasted, "chiefs of the army, the praetorian prefect, senators, we made all prisoners and deported them to Persia." Thus it is that in the vast stone relief at Naqsh-i Rustam, Valerian, the Roman emperor and Shapur's prisoner, is seen kneeling before Shapur, who grasps the wrist of another Roman ruler, probably Philip the Arab.

Upon returning from the wars to his native Persia, Shapur I built what its excavator, French archaeologist Roman Ghirshman, calls the Sassanian Versailles, Bishapur, or the "Beautiful City of Shapur," said to be an abbreviation of the aphorism "the city of Shapur is more beautiful than Antioch." There at the foot of a mountain, where the Shapur River cuts through a gorge and opens onto a fertile plain, Ghirshman and his colleague Georges Salles uncovered a number of buildings, including the cruciform hall of Shapur's palace and another edifice with exquisite floor mosaics. A dig by the Iranian Archaeological Service beginning in 1968 exposed its outer defense system of massive walls and deep ditches, and discovered a semisunken stone building thought to have been a temple. As many as 80,000 people are believed to have lived there.

*Two rock-cut Sas...
among the desola...
Rustam under a...
by Zoroastrianis...
burying corpses, ...
dead to carrion ...
they then placed ...
suaries. Cremati...
because fire was ...
portrayed fire al...
silver c...
rei...
o...*

flowed in from commerce and agriculture. Irrigation, an age-old technology in the Middle East, was expanded by the Sassanians, whose fertile lands produced rice, vegetables, and dates and other fruit. Roman engineers captured by Shapur I were used to design and build dams to control surface water. Sassanians may also have made many *qanats*, underground channels that tapped ground water and moved it to the surface, where it could be used.

Their control of the trade routes left the Sassanians in an enviable position, which they enhanced by increasing in length and complexity the road net of the old Persian empire. Commercial routes now included much more than the Silk Road, although that remained of primary importance. Caravans moved across the empire between trade centers in China, India, and Mesopotamia, and ships traveled along the Persian Gulf and Mediterranean coasts, carrying cloth, metals, oils, dyes, glass, food, wood, and gems.

The money-based economy underlying this commerce was good for business; but it was of more than monetary value 1,600 years later to German archaeologist Ernst Herzfeld. Paying close attention to old Sassanian coins when he began working there around the beginning of the 20th century, he discovered that each of the monarchs on the coins wore a distinctively different crown. Ardashir, for example, has on a skullcap topped by a globe of hair encased in silken gauze, and Shapur I wears a crenelated crown. In time Herzfeld and other archaeologists were able to identify the kings by their crowns.

Many of these Sassanian kings provided a barrier to the onslaught of the fierce warriors of the Central Asian Steppe. Huns, Vandals, and others who devastated northern Europe did not destroy the Mediterranean civilizations because of the Sassanian resistance. The Romans at various times recognized this service by paying the Sassanians for their role in safeguarding the security of Rome.

The enormous wealth of the upper-class Sassanians enabled them to enjoy lavish comforts, and their monarchs lived in true splendor. Nobles as well as the royal household acquired exquisite gold and silver table services; a number of these dishes and drinking bowls exist today, many of them housed in Russia's Hermitage in a collection begun by Czar Peter the Great in the 18th century.

In the last century of the Sassanian empire two of its most charismatic kings reigned—Chosroes I and his grandson, Chosroes II. Both were celebrated as great heroes in an 11th-century Persian work, the *Shah-*

A statue of Shapur I, carved from a stalactite, lies toppled by an earthquake in the cave near Bishapur where it stood for centuries. The figure—originally more than 26 feet from ceiling to floor—was reerected in the 1970s at the cave's entrance by restorers using cement as a substitute for missing parts, but the statue has since fallen again or been taken down.

namb, or *Book of Kings*, an epic poem based on ancient sources that interweaves Persian myths, legends, and historical events, including those of the Sassanian period. Chosroes I was renowned not only for his military and diplomatic skills but also for his justice and for alleviating the distress of poor villages with provisions of seed and cattle. He founded a university, and his chief minister, Buzurjmihr, is said to have invented the game of backgammon.

The ruins of the beautiful palace Chosroes I built at Ctesiphon, known as Taq-i Kisra *(page 138),* reveal the massive barrel vault of the king's throne room. The largest example of its kind, it soars to a height of more than 110 feet, covering a hall 80 feet wide and 160 feet long. The trappings of the room have been described in narratives and seen on artifacts. His throne, supported by winged horses and cushioned in gold brocade, was set at the back of the room behind a curtain, open only when he held audience. The huge silver and gold crown of his office was adorned with pearls, rubies, and emeralds. The crown was so heavy it had to be suspended above his head by a golden chain so fine that his visitors, kept at a distance, were unable to tell that the king was not wearing it. When people fell to their knees, it was upon silk rugs with a garden design that had been placed over marble floors.

A great warrior like his grandfather, Chosroes II is celebrated more for his lavish lifestyle than for his largesse to the poor. It is recounted in the *Shahnamb* that on one royal hunt he was accompanied by 300 horses with golden trappings, 700 falconers with hawks and falcons, 1,160 slaves holding javelins, and 1,040 more wearing armor and carrying staves and swords. Seventy chained lions and leopards were part of the imperial entourage, as were 300 men leading panthers. Sprinting alongside them were 700 gold-collared hounds, fast enough to seize gazelles on the run. The king's retinue also included 2,000 minstrels, each mounted on a camel and wearing a golden coronet, prepared to entertain the hunters with music.

The good life did not last. By the early seventh century internal dissension and a long, brutal conflict with the Byzantine empire left Sassanian Persia weakened. In AD 636, Arabs—powered by the new faith of Islam—swept into the Euphrates basin, routed the Sassanians in a three-day battle at Al-Qadissiyah in present-day Iraq, and captured Ctesiphon. Yazdigird III, the last Sassanian monarch, escaped, but in 642 at Nihavend, on the Iranian Plateau south of Hamadan, the Arabs won a final victory. Some accounts say that in this last battle the Sassanian peasant infantrymen had to be chained together to make them stand and fight.

Initially, the impulses of the new masters toward what was the most highly developed culture of their age seemed to be purely destructive. They melted down exquisite works of silver and gold to cast the metals into coins, and they battered into rubble an urban architecture that was unlike anything they had seen. Erich Schmidt, taking aerial photos of ancient Iranian sites in the 1930s, was aghast at the degree of destruction that could still be seen. He reported on "magnificent palaces turned into desolate ruins and cities into mounds and fields."

Before long, however, the Arabs began to show an appreciation for Persian literature and history, to embrace Persian modes of government and administration, to value and imitate Persian architecture and other visual arts. "Though the mosque replaced the fire temple," wrote Roman Ghirshman, "it was built on the lines of the ancient sanctuaries, and the palaces of Arab noblemen were adorned like those of the Sasanids. Whatever the material employed—glass, metal, textiles, wood, or stone—the Arab craftsmen copied indefatigably the time-hallowed motifs of the past." In the 10th century, Muslim rulers of Iran proved even more enthusiastic, soon adopting what they considered to be a Persian lifestyle and officially endorsing a rebirth of the Persian language. In the end, Muslims nurtured and spread the memory of Persia. Wherever Muslims penetrated other cultures, from the Iberian Peninsula to southern Asia, they transmitted the genius of Persia to a wider world.

TREASURES FOR THE EYE

Working with gold, silver, precious gems, and colored glass, Sassanian artisans created magnificent works of art. Under imperial mandate to exalt the king, they catered to a taste for the luxurious. To ensure royal satisfaction, Shapur II (thought to be the monarch at left) established a system that divided artisans into specialty groups. In turn, these were overseen by his appointed chief, who directed their work, inspected craftshops throughout today's Iran, and apparently controlled raw materials: Metallurgic analyses of many royal vessels suggest the silver is from a single source.

The artisans dazzled with their skills. They used gold sparingly (perhaps because of scarce native deposits), frequently as an enhancement. Able to solder separate molded pieces to the surfaces of objects for a raised, three-dimensional effect, they often highlighted the additions with gold foil. This technique was richly employed in the production of so-called hunting plates, which show kings clothed in full regalia engaging ferocious beasts in mortal combat. Sassanian monarchs would present such works to allies and neighboring rulers as reminders of their authority, valor, and prowess.

Sassanian art influenced civilizations from the Far East to Europe, and objects of Sassanian manufacture traveled over long distances as gifts or items of trade and plunder, winding up thousands of miles from Persia. The widespread adoption of Sassanian motifs by other cultures, as well as the looting of objects by graverobbers, has hindered precise dating and attribution. What is certain, however, is that 13 centuries after the fall of the empire, its treasures continue to delight the eye.

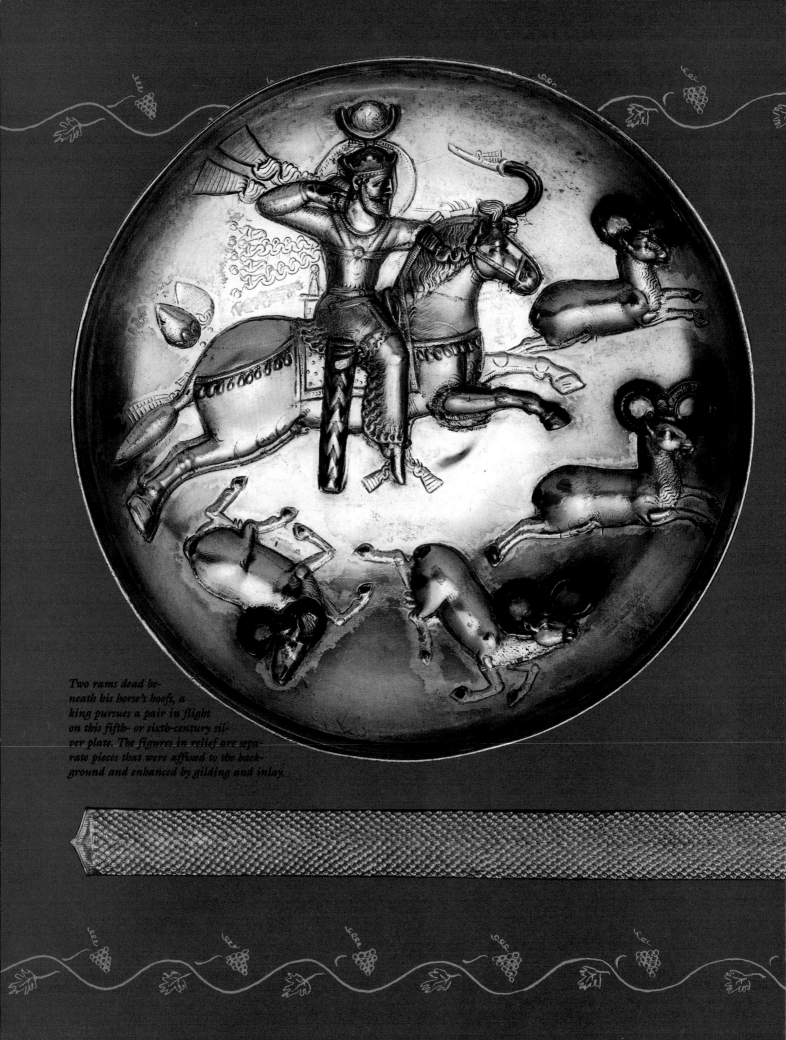

Two rams dead beneath his horse's hoofs, a king pursues a pair in flight on this fifth- or sixth-century silver plate. The figures in relief are separate pieces that were affixed to the background and enhanced by gilding and inlay.

In this third- or fourth-century-AD sardonyx cameo, a triumphant Shapur I, sword sheathed, grasps the arm of Valerian, signaling the capture of the Roman emperor. The piece commemorates the Sassanian victory over the Romans in AD 260.

Gold covers the scabbard and handle of this late-Sassanian iron sword, which is also embellished with inlaid garnets and glass jewels. Artists almost always depicted the Sassanian king with a sword, a symbol of rank and authority.

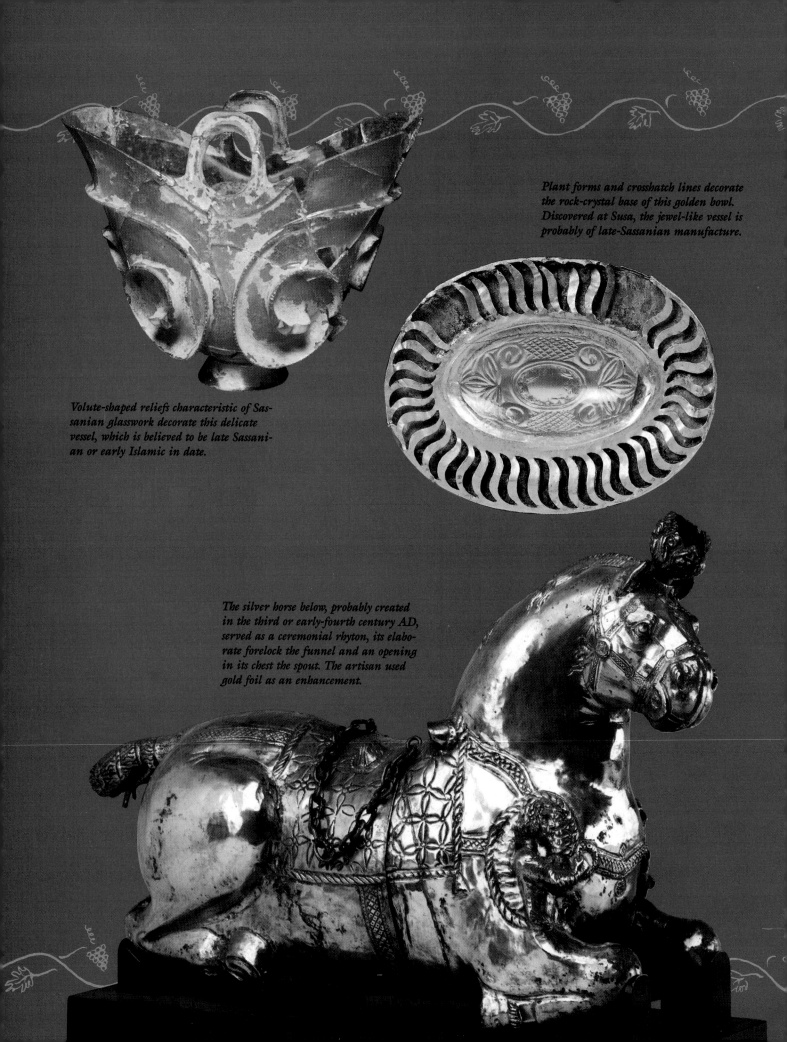

Plant forms and crosshatch lines decorate the rock-crystal base of this golden bowl. Discovered at Susa, the jewel-like vessel is probably of late-Sassanian manufacture.

Volute-shaped reliefs characteristic of Sassanian glasswork decorate this delicate vessel, which is believed to be late Sassanian or early Islamic in date.

The silver horse below, probably created in the third or early-fourth century AD, served as a ceremonial rhyton, its elaborate forelock the funnel and an opening in its chest the spout. The artisan used gold foil as an enhancement.

A male bird, surrounded by a halo and wearing a necklace with oval pendants, graces this seventh-century silver-gilt vase. In Sassanian art, such halos and necklaces are often associated with the king.

Semiprecious stones, called hyacinths by the ancients, still glow in their gold setting in this third- or fourth-century-AD belt pendant—thought to be of Sassanian origin—found in Wolfsheim, Germany, in 1870. A Persian inscription gives the owner's name as Ardashir.

Pouring liquid into the mouth of a tiny panther and holding a flower, a woman undulates on this silver-gilt ewer. Three similar dancers grace its other sides. Such quartets were among the most popular of late-Sassanian motifs.

A glittering rainbow of glass inlays encircles the rock-crystal center of this gold bowl, where a king, legs jutting in a typical Sassanian pose, is enthroned. Legend says it came to the Abbey of Saint Denis in Paris as a gift from ninth-century Holy Roman Emperor Charles the Bald.